Praise for *Writing While Masked*

"Individually and collectively their observations...are beautifully written, heartfelt and insightful pieces. They have brought their array of experiences, frustrations, sorrows, delights, comforts, and more to life."

—Marguerite Pappaioanou, DVM, PhD, Auxiliary Professor, Center for One Health Research, School of Public Health, University of Washington

"Each writing is an exploration of discovery, mystery, danger, worry, resiliency, and patience. The contributors responded to this experience from diverse angles and their engaging personal views give us what will be seen forever as an historical contribution."

—Yvonne Higgins Leach, author, *Another Autumn*

"Hats off to the seven women who spent the worst months of the pandemic writing, writing, and writing. They shared the honest stories of their lives, loves and fortunes and how they fared during those sometimes difficult and challenging times."

—Jean Godden, retired Seattle City Councilmember, former *Seattle Times* columnist, and author of *Citizen Jean: Riots, Rogues, Rumors, and Other Inside Seattle Stories*

Writing While Masked

Writing While Masked

OBSERVATIONS ON 2020 AND BEYOND

MARY ANN GONZALES

TYSON GREER

WANDA HERNDON

LAURA CELISE LIPPMAN

JANE SPALDING

SUZANNE TEDESKO

BETH WEIR

Basalt Books
PO Box 645910
Pullman, Washington 99164-5910
Phone: 800-354-7360
Email: basalt.books@wsu.edu
Website: basaltbooks.wsu.edu

An earlier version of this work was self-published by the authors via blurb.com.

Library of Congress Cataloging-in-Publication Data is available

Basalt Books is an imprint of Washington State University Press.

The Washington State University Pullman campus is located on the homelands of the Niimíipuu (Nez Perce) Tribe and the Palus people. We acknowledge their presence here since time immemorial and recognize their continuing connection to the land, to the water, and to their ancestors. WSU Press is committed to publishing works that foster a deeper understanding of the Pacific Northwest and the contributions of its Native peoples.

Cover design by TG Design

Contents

Foreword

GRACE CHRIST, PHD

PROFESSOR EMERITA, COLUMBIA UNIVERSITY SCHOOL OF
SOCIAL WORK

Disasters take people away and bring others together. *Writing While Masked* demonstrates this. It is an extraordinary book of how seven highly educated and remarkably accomplished women joined together to document their responses to and recovery from the coronavirus pandemic in its most acute phases. The book begins with the inception of the pandemic and extends through the distribution of the vaccine and more recent restoration of some semblance of normalcy in social engagement.

Written simultaneously with events as they unfolded, the group's descriptions of how they restored, reorganized, and ultimately restructured their daily lives to cope with the challenges of the pandemic provides an authenticity that is highly instructive and rarely available. The historical events themselves are carefully logged and give critical context for the reader. The integration of poetry with the description of activities provides an invaluable and sometimes entertaining insight into the authors' inner experience of these processes, including negative, angry, depressive and positive, joyous, even celebratory.

I was introduced to this writing group by two of its members, Laura Celise Lippman and Wanda Herndon, who were also members of a Seattle walking group to which I belong.

My professional life introduced me to trauma. I have served as a director of social work at Memorial Sloan-Kettering Cancer Center in New York and worked with people who have medical illnesses including cancer and AIDS.[1] After the 9/11 terrorist attack on the World Trade Center, I directed a long-term recovery intervention for widows with dependent children whose firefighter husbands had died in the terrorist attack. For over five years the Fire Department of New York (FDNY) supported the FDNY/Columbia University's home-based therapeutic program developed to mitigate adverse long-term effects of that traumatic loss for affected families.[2]

There are more similarities than differences between the process of recovering from a terrorist attack as compared to a natural disaster such as the coronavirus pandemic. Typically, disasters are analyzed in relation to the unique characteristics of onset, duration, scope, and degree of impact. The coronavirus pandemic has created a prolonged worldwide threat, profound and lengthy social and occupational disruptions caused by the need for isolation, and a social context in which older adults and culturally diverse people were at greater risk of death.

As I learned, differences in survivors' responses are often subjective. Trauma generally refers to immediate and continuing emotional responses to any perceived severe threat: loss of a sense of safety, of social connectedness, and of security, or challenges to one's assumptive world such as the current political and social conflicts that have emerged.

Three steps are said to comprise "reconstitution" from a traumatic or stressful event or situation: restoration, reorganization, and identity restructuring. These writers richly document how they transitioned through these adaptive processes and indeed are continuing to confront challenges and opportunities to this day.

Restoration: This phase includes identifying activities, travel, living arrangements, job demands, and social engagements to accommodate emerging information about the nature of the coronavirus threat. The challenge of restoration is as much emotional as practical. Where will you live? How will you connect/communicate with family and friends? How will you receive up to date and accurate information about your and your family's vulnerability/well-being? How do you cope with your feelings about so much change that requires isolation and separation from family, friends, work, and familiar activities? The seven authors document well the challenges of constructing such a "safe" environment.

Reorganization: This phase often includes a gradual routinization and feeling of comfort, success, and some satisfactions with accomplishments of the new structures. These included forays into nature, joys of cooking, gardening, acceptance of social limits, use of Zoom for maintaining family, friend, and work relationships and commitments, exercise, artistic productions, and other creative pursuits. There was relief that few friends and family had contracted the virus, i.e. the safe shelter was working. However, fears of the threat from social unrest and the combative political environment emerged.

Restructuring Identity: The third phase of restructuring of identity can most clearly be seen in the excellent postscript of this book. The vaccines were successful and enabled social contacts. New political leadership was met with huge relief and optimism as many felt able to advance life goals, relationships, and activities. The mood was celebratory with greater confidence about being able to meet society's political challenges and conflicts. This phase often includes a change in how one views oneself, one's identity: more independent, stronger, and successful, while at the same time individuals have a greater appreciation of their own and the country's vulnerabilities. One of the authors describes how exploring the roots of her family history in

New Zealand after vaccination brought her a welcomed perspective on their strength, survival, and contribution over generations.

Seven years after the 9/11 attacks I was asked to consult with a group of widows we had worked with previously and who had questions they wanted to discuss. During the meeting one woman announced that she thought she would break off with her current fiancé because of his inadequate support for her parenting of her sons. The other widows were quick to respond. "You are strong, you are capable, you have resources. If he is not providing the support you need, then you do not need him." They also expressed new acceptance when their sons wanted to become firefighters or to enter the military—occupations they had opposed in the early years after the father's death. "He died doing what he loved to do," they said, thus demonstrating how the perspectives of self, safety, and others can evolve over time.

This book provides a powerful guide to how the work of restructuring identity and gaining confidence and strength from meeting the challenges of such crises is a powerful process that is ongoing and continues to this day within a new context. As one author states, "Never again will I take for granted my freedom of movement, good health and ability to engage with the world."

July 2021

1. Grace Christ, *Healing Children's Grief: Surviving a Parent's Death from Cancer* (New York: Oxford University Press, 2000).

2. Grace Christ, Dianne Kane, and Heidi Horsley, "Grief After Terrorism: Toward a Family Focused Intervention," in *Grief and Bereavement in Contemporary Society: Bridging Research and Practice*, ed. R.A. Neimeyer, H. Winokuer, D. Harris, and G. Thornton (London: Routledge, 2011), 203–23.

Authors' Note

The process of putting our thoughts together on a page helped the seven of us weather the challenges of 2020. Some personal pieces written by individuals document what was being experienced right then. They are the writings of the moment.

Sometimes a moment is difficult to understand without access to its context. For that reason we have included information for each month in 2020.

Given life is lived and understood only with reference to what has come before, we have periodically included a rumination on what was reported. They are writings that reflect.

The writer Elizabeth George is correct in her observation that, "The past can't be changed, can it? It can just be forgiven." For this reason we have added in our thoughts about what we learned and what we want for the future. These are the writings of hope.

Who Are We?

We are a group of seven writers who meet almost every week at one o'clock for two hours. We have been doing this for a number of years now. Prior to the pandemic we gathered in our homes and the hostess of the day provided minor snacks and coffee. In March of 2020, we Zoomed until the weather warmed. Then we met outside, usually in Mary Ann's yard, masked, socially distant and without snacks, but rejuvenated beyond measure. In late fall when the rains came, we reluctantly returned to Zoom screens.

We are all retired from professional careers and, currently, from our shared passion of traveling. Some are grandmothers, some like to watch birds and plays. Others sew or garden. No one claims to be a gourmet cook—hence the modest snacks. All love to read and to laugh. We do that often.

The point of meeting is to discuss the writing we've done in the week prior. Those of us who have something written will read it aloud and the group members give their opinions. We also ask questions to provide the writer a scaffold for revision:

"Why did she say that...it seems out of character?"

"You said it was Tuesday on page two and Wednesday on page three."

"I want to know more about..."

"I don't follow..."

Since one of us is a poet we have different questions for her.

"Is that a made-up word?"

What we have learned over time is that all comments about your work are valuable, even the ones you don't like. Experience has taught us that, more often than not, the speaker is correct.

On our various writing journeys we have each displayed an imagination that has grown over time. It has been stretched by the very act of trying to structure something original and capture something ethereal, wonderful, quaint, sad or funny, in words. We have learned to look at the man who is oblivious to his ice cream cone dripping down his front, as a model for a clueless character in a novel. Better yet, we've seen how to make a humorous story about the mundane, such as a recalcitrant kitchen appliance. Some in the group who have not written poetry before have taken to writing it since the art form feels made for the moment.

Zooming our meetings is not as much fun since you can't hug first but at least we still see and talk to one another as a group. Worldwide, people struggle with isolation and loneliness, and feel compassion for the sheer exhaustion of the medical personnel and "essential workers" who put themselves at risk to save and to serve others. Adding to the woes of the year was an election that was chaotic enough in itself, but rendered more so by the virus and social unrest. It became harder to muster the mental wherewithal to sit alone and write but we had a "deadline" each week. That helped.

On May 25, the act of a white policeman pressing his knee to the neck of a Black man for eight minutes and 46 seconds was recorded by a seventeen-year-old girl on her cellphone. Other officers looked on with chilling nonchalance as he pleaded "I can't breathe." Her video of his death went viral.

The act struck a nerve with people who, for whatever reason, were finally weary of such gratuitous murders. The world, literally, exploded with protests in sympathy for George Floyd and with the Black Lives Matter movement.

At our Zoom meeting after the murder, we seven women recognized it as the cry of the unheard, the marginalized, the disrespected, and of those in deep visceral pain. Again, we faced the challenge of being able to write and were grateful when one member, Wanda, expressed her raw emotion in a poem called "I Cry." It offered us a means to cry ourselves and to grieve. "I Cry" was published in *The Seattle Times* on June 12, 2020.

We kept writing in a bid to maintain our balance in a world that had tilted sideways.

A Group of Seven Writers
During the Time of the Novel Coronavirus 2020

JANUARY 2020

JAN 2:   Australia calls third State of Emergency for bushfires in New South Wales. Koalas are being fed and given water in the wild

JAN 2:   Iranian General Soleimani is killed by US drone in Iran

JAN 7:   World Health Organization (WHO) notified of novel coronavirus emerging in China

JAN 8:   Prince Harry and Meghan Markle step down from duties as senior royals

JAN 8:   Ukrainian Jet crashes in Tehran, killing 176 people

JAN 16:   President Trump Impeachment Trial begins in US House of Representatives

JAN 20:   First US COVID-19 case identified in Washington state

JAN 23:   Wuhan, China, epicenter of outbreak of novel coronavirus, locks down

JAN 26:   Kobe Bryant and 8 others die in helicopter crash in Malibu, California

JAN 28:   Benjamin Netanyahu and Donald Trump announce Middle East Peace Agreement

JAN 31:   UK withdraws from European Union

In the Beginning

JANUARY 21, 2020

LAURA CELISE LIPPMAN

On January 21, 2020 the first person in North America with COVID-19, a newly identified human disease-causing virus first recognized in Wuhan, China, was hospitalized in Everett, Washington. Everett is the nearest city to the north of my home in Seattle.

My husband and I had planned a trip to meet our son and his family in Oaxaca, Mexico. We were to depart on February 16, 2020. By the time of our departure, cases had been identified in South Korea and Japan. The Chinese government found itself dealing with a full-blown epidemic. As physicians with close ties to the public health community, we knew that this hidden disease would probably be making its way to the United States eventually, likely through the airports, and we were aware of the close business ties that exist between China and Washington state, the home of the Boeing Company and Microsoft.

Our son, daughter-in-law and their two sons, ages 3 and 5, were nearing the end of a six-month sojourn in Mexico City. The boys had attended a Montessori preschool there, and their parents were working remotely at jobs in the states. Their original plan to spend Christmas in Oaxaca and enjoy the famous Festival of the Radishes was stymied by a flu outbreak that affected their little family. They had had to cancel their trip and they wanted to reschedule. We were meeting them for a redo, to help with logistics, babysitting and to enjoy the lovely weather, food and the renown arts and crafts scene there.

When we embarked for Mexico, I remember walking through the SeaTac airport with a heightened sense of caution; hand sanitizer was already in short supply at local drugstores. I had managed to score some, and we found unused sanitizing wipes from previous camping trips. I was hyper-alert; what was OK to touch, what contact should be avoided? Surfaces might be a problem on counters, and in bathrooms. What was the best way to open and close the doors of the stalls safely? I had facemasks left over from my clinic days (I retired from my family medicine practice years ago) and they were in my carry-on bag, ready for retrieval should I become aware of someone with a severe cough. I did have to ask myself why I wasn't always concerned about coughing near me; TB is airborne, and we had many case studies of transmission of that disease in med school!

We used a lot of hand sanitizer on our way through the airport, and once we boarded the plane, I wiped down the seats, armrests, and the fold down tables. I diligently wiped all the TV monitors. We listened carefully for sounds of respiratory disease, lest we needed to don our masks, but were satisfied there were none. Once we arrived at our destination in Mexico City and then Oaxaca, we observed the same precautions. We stayed at a grand old hotel on the outskirts of Oaxaca city with sprawling grounds, a nice restaurant and a lovely pool. We were so caught up in our reunion with our family and the beauty and fascination of Oaxaca that worries of COVID and precautions against catching it were forgotten. We visited ruins, crowded markets, museums, gardens and tourist shops. Occasionally I would look around me and wonder if somewhere the novel pathogen was lurking.

The vacation was a success, and it was our last foray out of the country. We, who have been inveterate birders and world travelers since our retirement over ten years ago. When we arrived back at the Mexico City Airport on February 25, 2020, a significant change was noticeable; luggage handlers, gate attendants and security processors were wearing masks and gloves. Hand sanitizer dispensers were at security checkpoints. There had been trickles of news from the US and Asia about growing infection rates. Again, we wiped down our airplane seats and readied our masks.

After uneventful flights, we arrived at Seattle customs and baggage late at night. There was no change of any kind at our home airport; no hand sanitizer dispensers, no temperature checks (I remembered those from the time of SARS), no masks or gloves on any attendants. It was a big shock after the change we saw in Mexico City! It unfortunately portended the denial of the disease that would unfold at a national level.

My son and his family had planned to make one last vacation visit; they had booked a family trip to Puerto Escondido prior to returning to their Seattle home. February. 29, 2020 brought the first Washington state area death from COVID-19. The day before my son's family was to leave for their grand finale Mexican trip, President Trump threatened to close our border with Mexico. My son conferred with us and decided to cut his visit short and come home rather than get stranded south of the border.

Their timing was unsettling! More local cases of the virus were identified on their return, and a scant three days after they returned to their home school, Governor Inslee initiated the Stay Home Stay Safe program and schools across the state were closed. I felt guilty that I had urged the kids to come home. The border did not close and Mexico was behind us in identifying cases—at the time it looked like they could have done better to stay where they were.

In the months to come of course, the pandemic struck both coasts and Mexico with vengeance. The virus and its prevention have been politicized and they are now symbols of cultural divide. The US has emerged with Brazil, India, and other unlikely companions as a poster child of bad management of epidemic disease. This has been particularly distressing to those of us with public health affiliations; watching the elite corps of the CDC quashed and its leaders capitulate to an erratic and irrational president has been heartbreaking. The CDC was a world leader of public health policy, education, and investigation. We can only hope it can reclaim its legacy, and that this pandemic abates soon.

FEBRUARY 2020

FEB 2:   Restrictions announced on US-China travel

FEB 3:   President Trump wins Iowa caucus for Republican nomination for president of the US

FEB 4:   Iowa caucuses results delayed due to quality control

FEB 4:   Diamond Princess Cruise Ship was unable to dock. Eventually over 700 people on board were infected by COVID-19; at least 4 died

FEB 5:   President Trump acquitted of impeachment charges by US Senate

FEB 7:   Lieutenant Colonel Alexander Vindman was removed from the National Security Council by Trump for testifying in House Impeachment Trial

FEB 11:   World Health Organization (WHO) names new virus COVID-19

FEB 11:   Justice Department overturns prosecution of Roger Stone's trial, giving a shorter sentence

FEB 13:   President Trump sends Rudy Giuliani to Ukraine to dig up dirt on Biden

FEB 24:   Harvey Weinstein found guilty of rape and first degree criminal sexual act

New York: Before it Started

FEBRUARY 15, 2020

BETH WEIR

People are astonished when Bruce and I tell the story of our 1972 helicopter ride across Manhattan and, if honest, we remain astonished as well. We were shiny newlyweds when we landed on a flight at Kennedy Airport from the United Kingdom. As part of our economy class ticket we had a free transfer to La Guardia Airport for our onward journey to North Carolina. It was night when we hung in the sky, the city sparkling below us, sending its magic upwards. Even jet lagged as we were, we applauded every landmark the pilot pointed out across the twenty-minute trip.

While it is hardly original to say so, the thing about New York is that the magic persists. It does so at both ground and helicopter level too over fifty years later.

Bruce and I flew from Seattle to New York in February—minus the helicopter ride. The winter wind would have sliced us in half, or worse, if we hadn't bulked up in layers and covered them with puffy jackets. New Yorkers toss off such weather in notable fashion and stride toward their business. Their greetings, cheerful and courteous, are often loud. The energy of the street performers could power another space shuttle if the country were still flying them.

My spouse and I were tourists for three days, among this exuberance and the windy canyons of the buildings of Manhattan. We walked the streets, taking in the main library, Grand Central Station, the Empire State Building, Times Square, Wall Street and...you get the idea.

On Sunday morning we explored Central Park, that magical and green 850 acres in midtown Manhattan. Along with the robins and people and cameras and horses with whom we were sharing the Park that morning, there were dogs. Collectively, they sprang along, tails waving like sails. Many were sufficiently obedient to be off-leash. One was a black terrier whose human mother untethered him after he barked at a squirrel. Once free, he took after it at high speed. At the moment he had the animal jammed up against the trunk of a tree, it turned and chattered angrily, waving its paws. The dog was startled and backed off. His owner laughed. "Loves the chase but never gets the catch."

Not a bad metaphor for New York I thought. It is worth the chase but, like the little terrier learned with the squirrel chase, you can never expect to catch it fully. Little did we know when we left the Big Apple that the corona virus was going to deny us any opportunity to return in 2020 to try once again.

Scrabble in the Time of the Coronavirus

FEBRUARY 25, 2020

BETH WEIR

As a retiree, with no children at home, my activities are not catastrophically disturbed by the shutdowns being enacted. Of course, my husband and I miss having plays in our life and chafe under a narrowing social life, but we are adjusting.

What has changed is that Bruce and I are practicing retirement since he has to work remotely. For the first time in our marriage, outside of travel, we are together 24/7. So far it is working, although you never know. My mother explained to me when she and my dad were visiting after he retired, "that sometimes I think your father and I made a mistake." This was from a woman I regarded as then having been happily married for over fifty years. There were no scripted responses at the ready to that remark. Since Mum and Dad made it to 60 years I guess she and my father adjusted.

Of course, my parents did not have the electronic distractions at the ready Bruce and I are enjoying. Virus or not we are still able to have our customary Friday night date with pizza and a movie at home. When we tire of binge watching we are able to resort to our default entertainment that so absorbed us when we had to mind small, sleeping children: Scrabble.

When we began playing Scrabble fifty years ago, Bruce kept score of each game and continued the custom. Now, when we unpack our Scrabble board from its battered, creaky box, we can examine the trajectory of our abilities. We have gone from wildly differing scores across games to consistently having totals as close as ink and paper. Presumably that represents growing skill over luck, but as our abilities matured our games became more intense. The recent one, where I managed for the first time ever to use every single tile on one word, comes to mind. All this virus time to play may throw us over the edge, which I imagine will happen when I manage to use all the tiles on a triple score!

In between we are giving some thought to how to celebrate our fifty years together next year. The ideas we are tossing about—a trip to Morocco, or to Antarctica—are just ideas at the moment but thinking about them takes us out of the sameness of our days. It is my hope that everyone has something special like that to look forward to; it is a great antidote to the cramped misery of the moment.

MARCH 2020

MAR 1:   Pete Buttigieg drops out of the US Democratic presidential race

MAR 1:   First known COVID-19 case identified in New York

MAR 2:   Amy Klobuchar drops out of the US Democratic presidential race and endorses Joe Biden

MAR 3:   Super Tuesday: Biggest voting day for Democrats selecting their presidential candidate revives Joe Biden's campaign; he wins nine states

MAR 3:   US Federal Reserve makes its largest rate cut in a decade, reducing short-term interest rates by 0.5% to protect economy against COVID-19

MAR 4:   Michael Bloomberg drops out of the US Democratic presidential race after a disappointing showing during Super Tuesday

MAR 4:   New study confirms human-caused climate change did make the 2020 Australian bushfire season worse, published by World Weather Attribution

MAR 5:   US senator Elizabeth Warren drops out of the Democratic presidential race

MAR 8:   America registers 521 cases of COVID-19 with 21 deaths across 33 states

MAR 9:   Italy announces it is locking down the whole country due to spike in COVID-19 cases with 10,040 cases and 630 deaths

MAR 10:   New York governor Andrew Cuomo deploys the National Guard to New Rochelle after one-mile radius zone established as 108 cases of COVID-19 detected

MAR 11:   COVID-19 declared a pandemic by the head of the WHO (121,564 cases worldwide and 4,373 deaths)

MAR 11:   11-year bull market ends as the Dow Jones industrial average falls more than 20%, temporarily, threatening to become a bear market

MAR 12:   President Trump bans travel with 26 European countries though not the UK due to COVID-19 (UK and Ireland added day later)

MAR 13:   African American Breonna Taylor shot and killed by police officers executing a no-knock warrant on her flat with a battering ram in Louisville, Kentucky

MAR 19:   With 910 cases of COVID-19, entire state of California ordered to "stay at home"

MAR 20:   Smoke from Australian bushfires killed more people than the fires—417 vs 33

MAR 23:   New York confirmed as center of the COVID-19 pandemic in the US with 20,875 cases (5,707 in the last day) and 157 deaths

MAR 23:   WHO says COVID-19 pandemic is increasing: first 100,000 cases took 67 days, 2nd 100,000 cases 11 days, 3rd 100,000 cases 4 days

MAR 26:   American cases of COVID-19 exceed all other countries, with 81,578 cases and 1,180 deaths (*New York Times*)

MAR 26:   Record number of Americans file for unemployment—3.3 million (US Department of Labor)

MAR 27: $2.2 trillion stimulus package passed by Congress, the largest in US history

MAR 30:   Three out of four Americans now ordered to stay home due to COVID-19 as states of Virginia, Maryland, Arizona, and Florida issue lockdowns

Together Again in the Shadow of the Plague

MARCH 5, 2020

LAURA CELISE LIPPMAN

We sit around the table
pass the Purell
and wash the children's hands excessively.

We look at our token wolf mask
in its place on the wall and
we howl the family howl

but only after we link hands, close our
eyes tight & say Grace,
my dead mother's name.

It's good to have us all back
from over the Southern Border
but I wonder about plague sequelae

& worry about the silent fetus
young & vulnerable &
susceptible to harm–

carried and so far safely.

The crown germ lurks and threatens
on every placid voyaged surface,
on every happy traveler's face–

its nonchalance a stark
contrast to the innocent porters
who shake its glitter indiscriminately
everywhere.

Being Immortal Is an Illusion

MARCH 14, 2020

BETH WEIR

At almost 72, I am in the demographic most at-risk for dying should I catch COVID-19. My physician friends have cautioned me that having survived this long means my system is, by definition, compromised. Sadly, it appears my still robust feeling of being immortal is an illusion. In any event, I have gone willingly into isolation at Washington Governor Inslee's urging to avoid being infected. Perhaps my ready compliance stems from the somber memory of my childhood neighbor, a family man with five children, succumbing to the 1953 flu epidemic. I was only five at the time but can still recall the palpable pall, grief, and fear around our street.

Washington State arrived early at the idea of keeping citizens homebound to keep them safe. Not that it had been a hard choice since the pandemic is upon us with outbreaks of COVID-19 decimating populations in Seattle nursing homes. We have the unpleasant label of a hot spot.

It is humbling to note that something way, way smaller than the diameter of an eyelash can tear up humanity all over the planet. This is the rare time that my generation has been asked to face a universal circumstance where no one, anywhere, is exempt. Many of us, particularly if we are white, and born in the West soon after WWII, have experienced generally rising prosperity and relative safety all our lives. The exception is the 2008-09 recession.

This was so for the generation born before WWI. My parents' story is likely close to typical. Both were eight when the 1918 flu made its rounds into their rural corner of New Zealand. They married at the depth of the great depression that preceded WWII and Dad served for three years in the army during that great conflict. After the war my parents developed a business; their first real chance to build for the future. Like many, they had to face down three events that were close to universal in their reach first.

I have become humbled when viewing my parents' history for lessons to aid navigating the current turmoil. Foremost is the respect I have developed for their resilience and continuing humor, born out of those experiences, as a way to cope. They taught me through example that it is better to start with a cold-eyed view of the way things are and to figure out from there how to enjoy or make better what you can. And you do that without whining.

When I have started to become restless in my new confinement, I try and remember their legacy. They were tested and prevailed. If you believe novelist Gail Sheehy, so will we. She said "To be tested is good. The challenged life may be the best therapist." It will be interesting.

Mindfulness

MARCH 19, 2020

SUZANNE TEDESKO

With no alarm to nudge me from slumber,
the morning light beckons;
falls in sword-like swaths across my bed.
I slide my fingers over the spread
following the lie of lustrous faux fur
and pull back the covers.

I sit up,
snag desiccated sleep from under a lid
and feel yesterday's Zumba ache
settle in my limbs.
Just noticing, not dwelling.

As the tea kettle burbles,
I peel a satsuma,
note the straggly white strands
that convene in the center.
Take my first bite
and the squirt of juice
jump-starts my brain.

I break two brown eggs
into the frying pan,
watch the not-yet whites fan out,
translucent and viscous,
while two yellow orbs
proudly stand their ground.
I await crisp white edges.
Just watching: no rush.

With time on my hands
I notice my hands.
Turn them one at a time
to observe my palms.
Which is my love line?
How long is my lifeline?

Stop!
Turn off the worry,
get back to the moment.
No drama, just noticing
on this now-channel day.

Pain Psalm

MARCH 19, 2020

LAURA CELISE LIPPMAN
Thanks to Catherine Wing

Pain be a goner from the heart
at the start let the heavy leopard
leap from my chest from my mind
from my gut ease the weight, the feral hate
the crate that squeezes the part
of my heart into dark, dark destroying fright
like a knife that cleaves and leaves me
limp and loose like a pithed frog
alone in its tray far from its
peers in the puddled pond among grassy
ferns and fetid stink. Let water stream
free, the blood race its pace through arteries
and veins in fleet flow, cascade and leap
with life to limbs and through the
plaque, hot pack the runways, runnels, run
free as can be along and strong
a body song of please and ease.
Through the portal over the mortal into
humors of the house that holds
liver and spleen those blood boxes of good
and grand metabolism catabolism
anabolism—enzymatic factories
of light energy and atoms alight
with zest of a thousand stampeding steeds
a million shining candles.

Letter to Virus-in-Chief

MARCH 20, 2020

LAURA CELISE LIPPMAN
Thanks to E. E. Lampman

If you have a secret
    keep it. Choose your
        targets like a heat-

seeking missile.
    Take out
        the perpetrator–

our orange-haired
    monster and his
        stuttery silver-tongued

accomplices—they don't
    know where or how
        to stop or start you.

Absolve the innocents
    and wise ones
        but take down

the disrespecters
    and dismissers.
        The world revolves and glows

as ICU monitors flicker
    and beep; germ-guns and bleach-bombs
        against you not yet discovered

or properly detonated
    against your crazy curated chaos.
        Ill-prepared sycophants

rail against
    mis-chosen enemies while
        proto-Nero fiddles at his wall.

During this conflagration
    the sun still shines
        the earth turns

and holds its center
    while invisible vectors
        writhe and gnaw.

We seers press back with isolation
    hope and determination
        to stymie defeat.

Vita Nuova

MARCH 25, 2020

LAURA CELISE LIPPMAN
Originally published in La Frontera

It lurks around us
spinneret jets flying to the dying
spun by the blades in the windy
gusts of universe

mixing it up
between the sum of us—the faithful
the faithless, the reds the blues
hues don't matter to

the nano-sized strands
of the micro-world
multiplying within us
without us

boring into our cells
helix by helix
zipper by zipper
fanning organelles
to hyper-energetic destruction

through the nares, the maw
into the lungs where self-
immolation and autophagism
collapse alveoli
into ground glass graves.

It Was COVID

MARCH 26, 2020

MARY ANN GONZALES

It was COVID that sent me into lockdown. It was COVID that provided a way to survive.

My daughter K.C. started me down this path. She brought me a pattern for a mask. She said her neighbor, a nurse, did not have enough N95 masks in the hospital. They were wearing cloth masks on top to lengthen the time they could wear the N95s. K.C. brought material and I had elastic.

Soon we had two hospitals for whom we were sewing masks to supplement the official supply. It was shocking and scary to me our hospitals were so unprepared. Where was the oversight that should be in place for just this kind of emergency? Soon, for the family and friends it became clear that we also needed masks to protect ourselves and others. K.C. continued to bring me fabric and I begged for more from friends and relatives.

A request had been made. "Anyone who could, please make 100 masks." There was no way I would be able to make that huge number, but just to goad myself into trying, I began a tally of how many left my sewing room. March 24, 2020 I began with a week-long count. Sixteen!

The original pattern morphed while we tried out better designs. It was clear the original design did not hold the material snuggly around the nose. We found a supply of coated wire in the garden supply at Fred Meyer. It was the best we could do at the time, but woefully inadequate as the wires twisted and poked.

The world of masks was evolving and soon we had aluminum nose bridges and better elastic. We could order fabric on-line and have it delivered. Amazing how different fabric looks on a small screen.

Being devoted to books, it is nearly impossible for me to pass one of the Free Little Libraries without peeking in. It was nearly cartoonish—a light went on in my head—what a great distribution venue. I have had few really great ideas in my life, but this was one.

Now, every day I take from 6 to 10 masks to the little box (with the homeowner's approval) and so far after 52 days, every day the box is empty. As a side bonus, I sometimes find little Thank You notes and occasionally a monetary contribution. I have chosen to be anonymous so the notes are often addressed to Mask Maker. I like that title, kind of Lone Ranger-ish.

So in the time of COVID, I know I am filling a need and being part of the solution. I am grateful to have a job. It keeps me busy and allows me to combat the sadness that seems to blow in on the breeze.

Italian Misadventure

MARCH 30, 2020

JANE SPALDING

So much anticipation for the trip to Italy. My fascination with things Italian began in 1973 when a help wanted ad in the Paris *Herald Tribune* captured my imagination. The American School of Milan had a vacancy for a first-grade teacher. I had already turned down two not quite right teaching offers, one in a school on the southern coast of Spain, and one in a high school on a military base near Pisa. A first-grade teacher? I could do that. In the largest city in northern Italy? Yes!

Now, in March 2020, when the world was largely ignorant about what was about to descend upon us, it was almost time to leave for a trip to Italy with my friend Trudy. The coronavirus was a faraway illness discovered in China. However, before the end of January, the first case in the United States was diagnosed in Kirkland, Washington, just across Lake Washington from my home in Seattle. Yikes! This really was too close to home.

Steeped in denial, we followed headlines and travel restrictions with a growing sense of unease. The week before we were scheduled to leave, we learned of a coronavirus outbreak in Northern Italy. Our two-week trip was mostly in the middle part of the country—a week in the hills of Umbria, followed by stops in Assisi, Florence, and Cinque Terra.

Would we go on March 11? Trudy, who is 81 years old and believes she can do anything, says to me, "I'm going, even if you decide not to." Her son and his wife, AJ and Natalie, were already there, living out a dream of spending five months in the hill towns of Umbria. Planning for the trip brought back memories of time in Orvieto, Todi, olive groves, fields blessed with poppies, and, of course, the world's best food and wine. Why would I not go?

We left on March 11, flew through Paris, and were met in Florence by a gowned, masked, and gloved woman holding a weird medical instrument to our foreheads. A normal temperature: we passed the first and, as it turned out, only screening of the trip. On to a week of touring the beautiful hills, eating the most delicious food. In a farmhouse in Calagrana that only served Sunday lunch we enjoyed a beautifully browned cheese souffle, a tiny dish of truffles on pasta, chicken with sausage and smoked carrots, and a perfect panna cotta.

I was in a Fellini movie. But our anxiety rose each day. Much of our news came from AJ and Natalie and their Italian friends who warned of an impending shutdown of the whole country. No longer was the virus contained to Northern Italy. Watching denial—"Oh they surely won't close the museums"—become acceptance. "We need to go home."

Trudy kept her good humor throughout. She walks with walking sticks and maneuvered the ancient, uneven walkways with grace. One misstep, I thought, and we could need medical care. A hospital in Italy is the last place I wanted to be. I've got to get us home. She is in the vulnerable age group. Then the realization, "Oh shit, so am I."

Hours spent waiting for a callback from Delta Airlines. Reservations made through Florence were cancelled the next day because the airport shut down. More hours waiting for Delta. We had to fly home through Rome.

The morning AJ and Natalie took us to the station in San Leo Bastia to catch a train to Rome, no one was out. The Italian government ordered everyone in the country to stay home. Anyone who had business being on the street must carry a form explaining their business. A young man in uniform stopped us when we got to the station of this tiny town. Thanks to their good friends who managed the bar/tabac/grocery/community gathering place in town, Natalie pulled out the required official form stating why we were on the street.

Rome was a ghost town, very light traffic and few people on the street. The first night at our hotel near St. Peter's Square staff from the hotel restaurant brought dinner to our room. The second night the restaurant had been ordered to close. That afternoon I walked the perimeter of an empty, barricaded St. Peter's Square. Every block or so, two people in uniform, the Italians do love their uniforms, stood beside the tiniest of European cars in front of barricades. I don't remember seeing any weapons. Finally, I found a convenience/grocery/liquor store that was deemed an essential service and got sandwiches and salad for our dinner. We ate in our hotel room while we watched the movie *Two Popes*. How absurd that we could see the same cupola from St. Peter's that was featured in the movie from our hotel window.

Early, early, the next morning a driver arrived to take us to the airport. Even in the pre-dawn hours lines were long. Confused passengers wandered about not knowing which line to stand in. About half of the airline counter service area had a uniformed person standing behind it. They appeared and disappeared as the line moved achingly slowly. Finally, it was our turn. I gave the man helping us everything I had, but I didn't have a confirmation number for my reservation. Without it he wouldn't give me a boarding pass. Trudy, who did have a confirmation number, took her boarding pass, and was whisked away in a wheelchair by an attendant. I was sent two terminals away in search of a Delta attendant who could give me the missing number with a warning that, "They don't usually come in before 8." Our plane left at 7:50.

Outside I ran as best I could pulling my luggage on wheels the distance between Terminal 3 and Terminal 5, the Roman home of Delta Airlines. Few staff, or anyone else, was in the terminal. Just as I was about to lie down on the floor and have a temper tantrum, an Italian man in uniform, said to me in beautiful English, "Mam, mam you are looking for Delta airlines? My colleague here works for Delta. They don't open till 8 o'clock but maybe he can help you."

This beautiful Italian Delta agent took all my ticket information and my passport behind an Employees Only door with only the words "Wait here." So, I waited, paced, tried the door a few times, felt utterly alone and deserted, thought of the long walk back to Terminal 3, and who knew how much of a longer walk to the right gate. Just when I was visualizing another temper tantrum on the floor, the Delta man appeared, thrust a boarding pass in my hands and said one word, "Hurry."

When I got back to Terminal 3 the lines were even longer. I searched the faces of those behind the counter. The agent who helped me earlier, who told me to come right back to him with the number, who told me he would be there all day, was not there! In desperation I turned to a Catholic priest who was next in line. "Good morning Father," I said, in my best Catholic school girl voice. I quickly explained my predicament and he graciously let me go in front of him. I learned he was from Michigan and had been in Rome on church business.

Next hurdle, the security line about a half mile away. A uniformed woman insisted that people keep a six-foot distance, even though we had been packed like sardines in the ticketing line. Who was at the front of the line? My Catholic priest who said, "Oh you again," and graciously gave me his place in front of the line. My guardian angel was on call that morning.

From there it was a dash to the gate, which seemed like at least another six miles. I checked in with the attendant, made sure I had enough time to go to the bathroom, and was the last one on the last flight out of Rome. I'm not totally sure about the last part of that sentence, but it was the day before flights from Europe were no longer allowed to land in the United States. Trudy was already seated wondering what happened to me. AJ and Natalie, who decided to cut their adventure short, were also on the flight.

Once on the plane, life was like normal. No one screened us at the Rome airport or at SeaTac. No one talked to us about quarantining. Caught in the head spinning changes the coronavirus pandemic caused as it erupted on two continents, we returned home to a very different Seattle than the city we left. We arrived home on March 19, three days after Governor Jay Inslee shut down schools, and all but essential services in our state, and told everyone to "shelter in place."

I couldn't help but contrast reaction in Italy and the United States. When the president of Italy ordered restaurants closed—boom, the next day they were closed. When the order came out that anyone on the street must have an official government form explaining why—people on the street had the form. In our rich country, with its lack of presidential leadership, so much fell on the governors. Everyone was scrambling to figure out what's next.

APRIL 2020

APR 1: All England Lawn Tennis Club cancels Wimbledon for the first time since World War II because of the coronavirus pandemic

APR 1: President Trump says the US Strategic National Stockpile is almost depleted amid widespread shortages of medical equipment to fight COVID-19

APR 2: Number of COVID-19 cases worldwide passes 1 million, with 51,485 deaths reported

APR 3: US aircraft carrier Captain Brett Crozier cheered off his ship after being fired for a letter demanding more help for his sailors infected with COVID-19

APR 5: Queen Elizabeth of Britain makes an address to the nation, "we will meet again," for only the 5th time in her 66-year reign

APR 6: Nadia, a tiger at the Bronx Zoo, tests positive for COVID-19, first known case of human-to-cat transmission

APR 7: US COVID-19 death toll passes 10,000 in six weeks, with more than 356,000 Americans infected. New York death toll reaches 4,758

APR 7: China ends its lockdown of Wuhan, the city at the center of the COVID-19 pandemic, after 76 days as the country reports no new deaths for the first time

APR 7: Australia's highest court overturns the child sexual abuse conviction of Catholic Cardinal George Pell

APR 7: US acting Navy Secretary Thomas Modly resigns after calling Capt. Brett Crozier of the USS Thomas Roosevelt "too naive and too stupid" in address to the crew

APR 7: Wisconsin holds its Democratic primary with in-person voting in the midst of the COVID-19 pandemic, after mail-in voting rejected by the Wisconsin Legislature

APR 8: Bernie Sanders drops out of the US Presidential race

APR 12: Huge storm system produces more than 40 tornadoes in the US from Texas to South Carolina killing 32 people across six states

APR 14:	Parts of Europe begin to ease lockdown restrictions after 5-6 weeks with some shops opening in Austria and parts of Italy
APR 14:	President Trump freezes funding for the World Health Organization
APR 16:	22 million Americans have filed for unemployment in 4 weeks
APR 19:	US coronavirus death toll passes 40,000, with 742,442 cases recorded
APR 20:	Georgia, Tennessee, and South Carolina first to announce end to at-home restrictions
APR 21:	President Trump announces new 60-day ban on most green card applications
APR 23:	At a White House briefing President Trump suggests injecting disinfectant as a treatment for COVID-19
APR 28:	US confirmed cases of COVID-19 pass 1 million, with a death toll of 58,365
APR 29:	US GDP falls 4.8% for the financial quarter; worst contraction since 2000
APR 30:	President Trump claims COVID-19 originated in a lab in Wuhan

Babies and Broccoli and Jack

APRIL 3, 2020

BETH WEIR

When our daughter arrived on this earth, I was paralyzed. I'd not ever been around any newborns. When I expressed my anxieties to the head nurse, a woman who'd experienced her share of wobbly, new mothers, she said, "Not to worry, the directions come with them."

A similar piece of advice offered about dealing with uncertainties comes from an old Mel Brooks comedy routine where he plays the role of a therapist. He cheerfully tells a patient, "Listen to your broccoli and your broccoli will tell you how to eat it."

Acceptance of this odd premise—which I confess amuses me—leads to the question of what next: how does one listen for directions from a baby or a stalk of broccoli? It also seems to me that the current lockdown in most of the world, courtesy of the coronavirus, is a kind of baby/broccoli occurrence. We have to listen to it. The next question is how.

Admittedly, we are getting directions from many quarters about how to behave. Most folks listen to the messages from people who have spent careers investigating transmissible diseases. Their faith in them is derived from a belief they know what they are talking about. Under their guidance, we are still in lockdown at this point.

Lockdown is not the Idaho way, one state senator has protested, according to a Facebook posting in my feed. It's unconstitutional not to let people gather to drink or go to church. There is a process Charles Darwin described that will take care of such folks. However, since giving the finger to the authorities also brings down the more constrained among us, the flaw in that thinking is obvious.

There is information being doled out regularly about masks, distancing, hand washing, etc. The official bulletins are necessary but not sufficient, since you're on your own after this advice has been dispensed. This is when you have to "listen" for your personal directions on how to behave in the time of COVID. Listening also means following the voice in your head that tells you how you should behave so you still like yourself when the restrictions are over.

In my case, I am adhering to the one thing the nurse would admit to when she told me I'd be fine as a mother. It was to stick to a routine. For that I have help from our scruffy terrier, Jack. He is three this month and has a well-honed order to his day that keeps me in line. He sleeps till 11:00 most mornings if I am quiet, on the sofa beside him, reading or writing. About noon he figures it's time and he lets me know that in his doggy way. We head off for our wander at socially acceptable distances from the other dog owners at the park. We are there a half-hour since I listen to a thirty-minute podcast as I walk. Jack has a great sense of when that time is done and is happily harnessed up for home. Once back he chases squirrels in the back yard while I garden. Bruce then throws the ball for a spell. Rinse and repeat.

Having said that, periodically Jack drags his doggy bed out into the living room and rips holes in it. I know how he feels. Particularly after hearing this week that Washington State will be closed for business for another month.

I am taking solace from the fact that our daughter is now grown and a cheerful, functioning adult. I will presume that means I followed her directions. Got to confess I haven't been able to deal with listening to broccoli quite so adroitly. However, I am growing it and weeding around the plant soothes my soul. Perhaps that is how it works. If I want robust broccoli I have to listen to its needs. In any event, working in the garden will get me through the miseries of the moment.

Looking on the Bright Side

APRIL 5, 2020

BETH WEIR

I think it is Day 18 of the lockdown. In any event my sense of humor is starting to desert me. Aside from Scotch, my go-to balm is writing. So ... after having written I am "balmed" up for a spell and am feeling a bit more optimistic. I can be persuaded to look for the bright side.

If you Google "Always Look on the Bright Side of Life" you will find a number of YouTube versions of the song. The song originates with Monty Python member Eric Idle and was first featured in Monty Python's *Life of Brian* (1979). It's been claimed by the public since then—is sung chorus fashion at public events such as football matches and funerals.

Listening to its lyrics that are simultaneously bouncy, funny, and morbid feels like a perfect reflection of what we are collectively living through. The song points out that somehow and inexplicably there is always room for humor among the cares of the moment. It is black or gallows humor.

Now that I am at Day 18 of lockdown, I am finding humor of any stripe is a champion way of coping. Am endlessly surprised by the cleverness of some of the Facebook posts relating to the coronavirus that come through my feed. The pithy expressions make me smile and sometimes laugh out loud.

Now that we have everyone washing their hands correctly.

Next Week: Turn Signals!!!

While everything is shut down maybe they should pave the roads.

After years of wanting to clean my house but lacking the time, this week I discovered that wasn't the reason. I know that last one, particularly, to be true.

Given I am not a Trump fan I have given up listening to the briefings from the White House in favor of those folks such as Governor Cuomo who aren't challenged when putting together a sentence and recognize the importance of correct information. I can mark that decision to my birthday when I heard Trump say: "There are a lot of people out there who haven't died yet." In fairness running an offensive against a virulent disease we had time to prepare for and didn't, cannot be easy.

The day after Trump's comment I saw another posting of three hillbillies looking confused. One turns to the others and says, "Have you ever listened to someone talk for a while and wonder if their cornbread is cooked in the middle?" Yep, I have. Evidently, I am not the only one to feel like this. Our local radio station (KUOW) has made an editorial decision not to stream Trump's coronavirus briefings live on the grounds he tells too many lies. The information he announces put people in danger. This is not hyperbole as one man died recently in Arizona following Trump's advice to use hydroxychloroquine.

Personally, that decision by the radio station made looking on the bright side of life a bit easier for me. So does the weather. Spring is upon us and I can spend as much time as I want—which is pretty much all day—among the rising greenery. When in the front yard I am able to have live conversations with people who are taking their daily decompression walk. (At the dog park, folks call that getting out the zoomies.) Truth is, I would be hard pressed to tell you what was discussed in any of my chats but that is beside the point. The fact they are happening makes you want to look on the bright side of things. There is one caveat. We do have to shout a bit so those of us in the vulnerable population groups, who are likely to be wearing hearing aids, can hear when six feet away.

Bread in the Time of COVID

APRIL 17, 2020

TYSON GREER

Back when I lived in a tiny adobe house in New Mexico and my sons were a babe in arms and a toddler, I made sourdough bread twice a week. In the cheerfully rolling chaos generated by two small sons, it was a routine I enjoyed (though I've never been one to look forward to routines). Folding in the fourth or fifth cup of flour was hard but satisfying work. This was before bread machines.

Watching the bread's first rise, seeing it swell above the blue ceramic bowl, felt like expectations fulfilled. The rhythm of kneading the bread, pushing and folding the dough again and again and again, felt good to my arms and shoulders. The aroma of baking bread made the house seem to swell with pride. Every step in the process was satisfying, but none as much as savoring the first warm, buttered slice.

Now my boys are grown men, 55 and 52. Why had I stopped? I don't remember.

Buying bread for Jim, with his impressive array of allergies, has been challenging for 30-odd years. But we've managed. So, in January of this year, it wasn't scarcity that prompted me to begin making bread again. I just felt like it.

A half-full, squat jar of yeast had been biding its time in the fridge. The bright red Kitchen Aid mixer stood ready to pummel in that last cup of flour. I bought several kinds of flour, hauled out the mixer, added two and a half teaspoons of yeast, a cup and a half of warm-to-the-touch water, and a tablespoon of molasses and watched the potion swell with expectations.

Expectations are funny things. Before we were ordered into "lockdown" or "to shelter in place"—the second phase has a nicer ring—and before COVID-19 was declared a pandemic, anxious shoppers stripped grocery shelves bare. It was shocking to see four rows of empty shelves in the baking section of one supermarket, and another, and another.

By March, the internet nearly burst with recipes for "easy" and "no knead" bread, and people discovered they could do it. Even rye flour, spelt flour, almond flour, and potato flour became hard to find—and, after the stores realized that hoarding had become popular as a pandemic pastime, shoppers were limited to two bags of flour, if they could find any. ("There is a fine line between hoarding and storing," my L.A. son remarked.)

Twice a week, more or less, I baked bread and watched the level of my precious little jar of Red Star Active Dry yeast slip lower and lower. I asked friends and family members, "See if you can find yeast. Any kind." No luck. An internet search yielded dire results: "No product within 100 miles."

Fortunately, back in December 2019, a member of my book club had offered to share her sourdough starter—she'd been baking up a storm—and on April

4th, I jumped at the chance. On that cold, rainy night, I drove a mason jar home with four precious ounces of starter. Experts agree naming your starter helps you develop a relationship with it...him...her.

Naming a baby is hard enough. I went to the "name store" again and again, looking for a name that was both literary and timely. Jim suggested (he had a large, vested interest in the outcome) I name it... him... "Ovid."

My first week with Ovid, as with all new babies, was challenging. Like a child, a starter needs to be fed and insists on a routine. Twice a day. Actually, every 12 hours. (One time, when my schedule drifted, I did wake up at 4 a.m. and fed him.) There were at least two anxious phone calls between me and the reassuring book club member.

Of course, feeding Ovid 4 ounces of flour and 4 ounces of water every 12 hours, means creating jars and jars of little-Ovid. My kitchen began to feel like the set of "The Sorcerer's Apprentice." The surplus "weak" starter went into crackers, pancakes, biscuits, waffles, muffins, scones—anything that could be baked.

By the second week of April, Ovid was still too "weak" to manage the task of bread rising on his own. (Turns out, I could have been brought up on charges of starter abuse, as I was starving Ovid—but that's too long a story.) Using the training wheels approach, I baked bread with a combination of Ovid-starter and 1 teaspoon of the dwindling yeast.

By the third week of April, the yeast jar was nearly empty, and Ovid still wasn't robust—one week left of hybrid bread.

Something I've discovered about COVID-time is that although we may have to keep our distance, kindness knows no boundaries. One day, when my neighbor to the north and I were chatting across our decks, I bemoaned my situation, and she offered, then delivered (with gloves and right to my door-step) a plastic baggie of yeast from her Costco supply (no longer available) in her freezer. It kept me going.

Some loaves later, talking to our friends in Idaho about being yeast-less in Seattle, they noted, "There's plenty in our stores." In two days, I received a small package in the mail—a squat jar of Red Star Active Dry yeast. Now, if Ovid is feeling punky, I have the luxury of alternate ways to make bread, scones, biscuits.... But like adopting a child, then having a surprise one—since I have yeast, Ovid has been feeling fine.

So twice a week, more or less—I am retired, and can say no to routines—our house comes alive with the fragrance of baking bread.

I make sandwich bread for Jim and small seedy rolls (a.k.a. squirrel food) for me. Deep breathing while punching, pummeling, pulling the dough and making "ring-and-run" deliveries in the neighborhood are my best antidotes for the infectious lies spewed from the White House and the latest COVID numbers.

When I think about the distress over yeast or no yeast—or Ovid working or sulking—I'm acutely aware of how extremely lucky Jim and I are. We are in good health and fit. We are retired, don't have jobs to go to/or not go to/or lose; don't have toddlers or teenagers to manage; and do have family and friends who offer to pick up groceries for us, including flour. We are so fortunate. I feel that sense of fortune twice a week—more or less—when I glide into the rhythm of baking bread, a surprising benefit from the time of COVID.

A Thank You to Wordsmiths

APRIL 23, 2020

BETH WEIR

As a lover of words, I feel fortunate we have a lot of them in the English language: north of 500,000. Better yet, since they can be reused often we are not in danger of running out of them and, if you don't like a given word, you can always tap into the thesaurus and get another. For example, if you are tired of hearing that this virus is still a mystery, you can substitute puzzle, enigma, conundrum, riddle, secret or problem. Now, none may have the particular nuance you are looking for but you can't complain about not having options.

The current shut-in time has meant that many people who like language as a job or an avocation have come up with some clever word constructions on Facebook. My favorite to date is:

> The spread of COVID-19 is due to two factors:
>
> 1. How dense the population is
>
> 2. How dense the population is

I am in awe of people who dream up such clever, crispy comments.

If there is an exception to my affection for words, it is the one getting a significant work out every night on the news at this moment. Unprecedented. It means it has never happened before. Certainly it is hard to argue with the high usage by reporters in these turbulent times. All the same, its use is starting to wear thin.

This has led me to think what else people reporting on the pandemic can say if the use of unprecedented were to be discontinued. Like most words it does not have a complete equal. Those tend to die out. However, it does have some close companions: unheard of, unknown, novel, unparalleled to name some. The substitution I like the most is unexampled.

I was knee deep in this issue of alternatives to unprecedented when my husband and I began following the show *Ozark*. The story is droll and strangely addictive but the language barely keeps up. There is not one character who speaks a sentence without using fuck as noun, verb or adjective. If you removed such words from the script it would be half the size. Since I don't have any particular aversion to the word and its familiars, what is the problem?

Fuck, like unprecedented, is overused and now without any emotional impact. It feels more like breadcrumbs on the counter. Irritating. What it does mean is that while fuck is being employed, viewers are not being exposed to the glories of the other 500,000 words that could be used in its place. Sadly, the show is not unprecedented in its aversion to the richness of language. In this particular case I do think one of the synonyms—unexampled—works better.

For all my fussing, I have made my peace with unprecedented since there is no other word that works as well in these times. Maybe I am tagging it unfairly because it is typically used in a negative context and cues for yet more bad news. What does save me are the cheeky wordsmiths out there. The cryptic remarks perform at least two laudable functions: making us laugh and keeping up our awareness up of the glories of language. For that I am grateful.

Unexpected Cohabitation

APRIL 28, 2020

JANE SPALDING

The need to know what happens next. My choice on the last Sunday of December when our minister invited us to select one thing we wanted to leave in the old year, infuse it in a rock, and drop the rock into a bowl of water. This act symbolized my desire to live in the moment in 2020.

What a forewarning!

In mid-March, when our governor declared a lockdown, Nick, who I've been dating for a year, invited me to isolate with him at his farm on Whidbey Island, an hour from Seattle where I live. It wasn't a "come up for a day or two" invitation. No, this invitation had conditions. "Move in until the lockdown order is relaxed. No going back and forth to Seattle. Bring some things you'd like to do while you're here," he said.

Nick is 74; I'm 72. We met on match.com one year earlier. He made it clear in our first conversation that he wasn't ready for a monogamous relationship. He was still grieving his deceased wife of eighteen years. We agreed to meet for lunch anyway. And here he was inviting me to move in?

"Pack like you're going away to college," my brother advised. Except going away to college, you know how long you're going to be there and have a shorter lifetime of baggage to sort through. This felt more like running away from home. Leaving my own home, my daughter, my friends and community to settle into a beautiful island home for an undesignated amount of time?

Now after being here for 2 months, I know it was the right decision. An early conversation about "this is not forever, is not a commitment," diminishes the need to know what's going to happen at the end of lockdown. An unknown number of tomorrows takes the urgency out of our lovemaking. We create an elegant choreography in the kitchen.

And I'm learning to live in the shadow of Nick's wife, who died nearly three years ago. Can you develop a relationship with one who has passed on? I know I would have liked her. A people magnet, the brains behind the masterful gardens they created, a loving grandmother, writer, knitter, cook, pretty much an excellent fill-in-the-blank person. She and I even shared the same profession. We raised funds for hospitals and educational institutions.

Now, using her hair dryer, cooking in her well-equipped kitchen, sleeping in her bed, seeing her photo first thing in the morning all seems a strange kind of intimacy with someone I'll never meet. I've yet to find a how-to-book on moving into the home of a beloved late wife. As far as I can tell, it takes acceptance, appreciation, and a rooted sense of self. Of course, I know I can't be her. I can only add my spirit to their home and let it roll off when he occasionally calls me by her name.

What happens next? I don't know. But every day I'm grateful for a wonderful shelter-in-place companion as we grieve and wait out this global tragedy. And I'm grateful I can still button my jeans.

MAY 2020

MAY 4:   A highly venomous hornet species from Asia, "Murder Hornets," reported in Washington State

MAY 6:   Video footage just released of an unarmed Black man, Ahmaud Arbery, being gunned down and killed by two white men while jogging in a Georgia neighborhood in February

MAY 8:   The Bureau of Labor Statistics reports the largest one-month decline in employment and the highest unemployment since data collection began in 1948

MAY 16:   Former US President Barack Obama delivers a virtual commencement address to millions of high school seniors

MAY 20:   As states begin to reopen, the CDC announces guidelines for communities, schools, workplaces, and events to mitigate the spread of COVID-19

MAY 24:   President Trump issues a travel ban against Brazil due to that country's rise in coronavirus cases

MAY 25:   George Floyd dies in police custody following his arrest after a Minneapolis police officer uses his knee to pin George Floyd's neck to the ground for nearly nine minutes

MAY 26:   Protests begin in Minneapolis, highlighting the #blacklivesmatter movement. The four officers present at Floyd's detention are fired

MAY 27:   Protesters throng streets around Minneapolis's Third Precinct police station, chanting, "No justice, no peace" and "I can't breathe"

MAY 28:   Minnesota Governor Tim Walz activates the National Guard

MAY 28:   The CDC reports that over 100,000 people have died of COVID-19 in the US

MAY 29:   Derek Chauvin, the officer who held Floyd down, charged with third degree murder

MAY 30:   Protests erupt in at least 30 US cities over the death of George Floyd

MAY 30:   President Trump announces he is cutting US ties with the World Health Organization, claiming the WHO is a "puppet of China"

MAY 31:   Demonstrations across the country erupt into arson and violence in the evening. A truck drives into protesters in Minneapolis. National Guard troops are called in to over a dozen states

Finding Joy in the Time of Virus

MAY 15, 2020

JANE SPALDING

"Shelter in place," said the governor of Washington.

"Move in with me and we can isolate together," said my friend Nick. Unexpected cohabitation was the result. I left my home in Seattle the end of March, drove to Nick's home on Whidbey Island, and moved in.

One silver lining in this quarantine experiment is that Nick and his wife, who died nearly three years ago, created an exquisitely furnished kitchen with every modern culinary toy invented. Soon after I arrived, I was looking for a hand mixer. He introduced me to the Kitchen Aid, a marvelous machine that whirs, whips, shreds, spiralizes, shapes pasta, and turn vegetables into noodles. Nick, who is a natural tinkerer of things mechanical, flips attachments with ease. He goes from whipping egg whites to grinding cabbage into slaw, all in the kick-ass Kitchen Aid in the blink of an eye.

Some of the gastronomic tools that have taken up residence in his kitchen include a food dryer, a meat grinder, an apple peeler, a juicer, and an ice cream maker. These outsized electric devices, with their hooks, blades and protrusions, bring to mind a medieval torture chamber. They've stood guard in their places on open shelving during my, going on three-month, reign as a slightly intimidated queen of the kitchen.

The true gift among all these food preparation instruments is the Instant Pot, a modern-day pressure cooker. The Instant Pot looks like a model for an early version of R2-D2, without the arms and legs. Or maybe it was the other way around. After all, R2-D2 came first. Williams Sonoma, in tribute to the newest Star Wars movie, is actually offering, via curbside pickup, Chewbacca, Stormtrooper and Darth Vader lookalike versions of an Instant Pot. This marvelous machine offers seven functions in one pot: you can cook rice, steam, slow cook, pressure cook, sauté, make yogurt and keep food warm.

The only thing I knew about pressure cookers prior to March, was my mother used to cook a whole head of cauliflower in one. I watched wide-eyed with awe and trepidation as the mysterious cooker steamed and the silver bobble on top bounced around. Eventually she lifted the whole cauliflower out and covered it with the most delicious creamy Velveeta cheese sauce. Ten-year-old me was sure eating this must be what you do in heaven.

One day a package arrived in the mail containing a book called *Indian Instant Pot Cookbook* by Urvashi Pitre. Unbeknownst to me, Nick ordered it as his way of saying he'd like his version of comfort food. He has a rich Indian heritage, as his grandfather owned a coffee plantation in India and his mother grew up there. He had been putting up with my version of comfort food, all potatoes and cheesy pasta and ground beef combinations, while secretly longing for Indian food. A new cookbook, an Instant Pot, time, and a willing human subject opened a whole world of cuisine I knew very little about.

The spices! Oh, the spices! Garam Masala: to make this starting place of Indian food one can combine coriander seeds, cumin seeds, whole cloves, cardamom seeds, bay leaves, red pepper flakes and cinnamon sticks in a spice or coffee grinder. Or find a jar in the pantry as we did.

Chicken Biryani was the first dish we made. We sautéed Garam Masala, onion, ginger, garlic, jalapeño chilies in the Instant Pot before adding chunks of chicken to sear gently on all sides. Once the chicken was nestled among the spices, cilantro, mint and rice went in. The whole mess was covered in a cup of water, the lid locked into place, buttons set on Manual and High Pressure. How long? Five minutes! Then you have to wait for the little silver button to drop down, indicating the pressure has released, while smelling the deliciousness. Final instruction of the cookbook—"Open and inhale deeply the true-to-tradition aroma of the dish!"

Shrimp coconut curry was next up, but it wasn't until we got to the Chicken Tikka Masala that I was hooked! After the first bite I said, "I never imagined I could make something so delicious." The sauce coated each piece of chicken brilliantly, and the combination of spices, creaminess and Basmati rice made every bite a delectable burst in the mouth.

Cooking has become my way to cope with this vast and rapid society-wide upheaval of 2020. Fortunately, I've come a long way from my early days of craving anything with Velveeta cheese. And I didn't follow a tip from my sister who called one day while we were in the middle of making an Indian dish. Her advice? "Put about one quarter of the spices called for in the recipe, or you won't be able to eat it."

I'm grateful for a shelter-in-place companion who is willing to chop anything and has the right appliance to do it. This week we're taking the Instant Pot to Mexico for Green Chili Stew. My thinking about food in heaven is evolving.

Mid-afternoon Malaise

MAY 19, 2020

SUZANNE TEDESKO

The "shoulds" police
swarm from every cranny,
converge on me
like army ants on the march;
adjudicators
dishing out
self-righteous scorn
wag their frosty fingers
mouthing tut-tuts.

I lie curled under a blanket
on the living room couch
as the minutes tick by,
hours, days
with dust to corral,
meals to prepare,
plants to water,
weeds to extract,
emails to answer,
papers to read.

But the swarm
of soft pillows
and this ceaseless sequester
beg me and my body
to stay put
and nap.

Suspension of the Moment

MAY 20, 2020

BETH WEIR

In a news clip I heard Arundhati Roy, the Indian writer of melodious novels, describe this time of the virus as one of suspension. In other words the past is stalled, the future is uncertain and the time in between, the right now, is still and quiet and allows for contemplation. In a sense the present is not going anywhere and the past cannot inform it. Her insight sheds light on why Roy is a Man Booker Prize winner.

I feel her characterization of the moment in my being during the daily mental health walks I take with Jack, our three-year-old terrier. To get our wrinkles out we sometimes go to a place where the relationship between the walk and the sniffing opportunities are high. That would be the small local dog park. Sometimes we walk where I prefer to go. That would be my neighborhood or the Burke Gilman Trail, three blocks from home.

What is true of these suspended times when there is little traffic is that the daily walks are placid. As such, it encourages the enjoyment of the spontaneous street theater encountered. In normal times the small dramas may have remained unnoticed.

The warm spring day I was wearing a floppy, red, sun hat comes to mind. I was visited by a hummingbird bent on sipping from it and confused when he could not. He stared at me at eye level, left, and came back again twice more, clearly frustrated. I had never been chastised by a hummingbird before and can now attest it is a possibility. There is also the case of the gentle 150-pound dog who stood on my foot and leaned against me in the dog park, not letting me pass after I had a social distance chat with his owner. The animal was a herder by nature and thought I now belonged in his pack.

In addition to uncovering the small dramas of life, human contact is a bonus. Its need for gratification is evident in the spontaneous "hellos" and exchange of small pleasantries when passing complete strangers. Likewise, people who walk by when I am gardening in the front yard will often stop and ask me what I am doing. I would guess few really are interested in the fact I have a lion's head maple tree. That is not the point.

Such actions help satisfy our needs for human interaction but they are also a tease, like a movie trailer. At each walk you get a glimpse of human contact with the caution that the full "monty" won't be yours for a while yet. But, every so often you get to have a substantial treat as part of the modest walking regime. Almost the whole movie. That happened last week when I stepped into a street I don't usually include in my rounds.

The street has city-planted trees in the parking strip that are substantial enough to hold the weight of both a hammock and a small occupant. Strung up in between two such trees was a fabric hammock, clearly occupied. The user was buried deep in the folds and covered over by the edge of the fabric. I followed my custom of pointing out things to Jack by saying that someone had found a good hiding place. Then a head popped up into the open. It belonged to a boy of about eight with apple-red cheeks. He was clutching a book in one hand by the author Rick Riordan. As a former reading teacher I was ecstatic to see a child reading, period, and more than pleased by the complexity of the text.

"Oh!" I said, "What are you reading?" It is impossible for me to do otherwise. The child grinned. "Greek myths!"

"Lovely," I told him and meant it. "Are they good?"

He nodded before sliding back down to his own world both within and without the hammock.

That little adventure counted as the whole film in these suspended times.

To Mask or Not to Mask

MAY 25, 2020

TYSON GREER

That is the stupidest question I've heard this year.

Let me rephrase the question: Whether 'tis nobler in the store to protect others and yourself or stand and scream at the top of your lungs that you have a Constitutional right to be a selfish idiot?

More Questions:

1. Do anti-maskers wear seat belts? Or do they chop them out of their cars and burn them on the courthouse steps declaring their right...to sickness and death?

2. In the dark nights of the WWII blackouts, did any Londoners raise their blinds and shout, "Bollocks! I'll turn on my bleeding lights if I want to!"

To accommodate ANTI-MASKERS, we have provided a space 40 feet west where you can stare at your reflection in the window since apparently you're the only person you care about.

Relentless

MAY 30, 2020

LAURA CELISE LIPPMAN

It was raining virus when my son went into the rain into the deep dark woods where the thunder struck and the lightning ripped and he stayed and stayed while the rain hit the mosses and the lichens, and their fruiting body tips. He could have sipped rain from the leaves and the furry cups of forest, the hairs of the bear in the rain with him, beware it came so close. The boys and I and his wife, we watched the huge drops hit the water and drip from tiles and drum the metal roof through the whole nights announcing rain, rain while he was out and then the rainy riots on the streets filled the airwaves with rain while the wash of the waves crashed the bulkheads with no sign of my son, their father, her spouse, he was by the river as the rain rained and the river ran higher and lakes got deeper and the skies stayed grey for days and black for nights. The towhees and swallows stayed silent, the sparrows stilled their voices and even the owls quieted while I came undone and the rain stormed and the storm reigned until the high of the mountains turned white when it cleared. The ferries continued their metronome journeys and my son, my son, my son arrived before the new curfew.

Is It Not Enough?

MAY 30, 2020

SUZANNE TEDESKO

Is it not enough
to have as our 'leader'
a narcissist, tyrant, liar and racist,
a blamer, a bully, a chauvinist thug
surrounded by sycophants
fueling bigotry and fear?

Is it not enough
to be shuttered inside
as a pernicious enemy
threatens our doors?
A global incubation
indifferent to borders,
religion or race
infects needed workers
who labor in close quarters
unshielded, untested.

Is it not enough
that our divider-in-chief
berates plagued governors,
touts fanciful cures
while his acolytes pack heat,
flout public protocols;
and elsewhere sick elders,
disconnected from loved ones
must die alone?

Is it not enough
that mom-'n-pop shops
go belly-up,
domestic abusers prosper
in crowded quarters
where children go hungry
and rent is past due?

Adding insult and injury
police violence erupts
in the streets in broad daylight,
blatant racism laid bare.

Licensed warriors
with assault weapons
sanctioned and lethal
snuff out a Black man—
knee-jerk bias
and adrenaline
fueling their acts.

Different names,
different places
but identical outcomes:
another Black death,
a hand slap for the cop
and likely acquittal,
no justice for the victim.
Is there no price for a life?

JUNE 2020

JUN 1: Protests over racial injustice spread overseas to Amsterdam, Spain and Nairobi among other cities. Forty cities across the US impose overnight curfews in order to quell the violence

JUN 1: Riot police shoot rubber bullets and tear gas into peaceful demonstrators in Washington DC's Lafayette Park to clear the park for President Trump's walk to St. John's Episcopal Church where he posed for a photo op holding a Bible at the historic church

JUN 3: Three former Minneapolis police officers implicated in Floyd's death charged with aiding and abetting second-degree murder and manslaughter

JUN 4: Police in Buffalo, New York, are suspended after video shows police shoving a 75-year-old man to the ground with his head bleeding

JUN 4: Virginia Governor Ralph Northam orders removal of a statue of Confederate General Robert E. Lee from the state capital at Richmond

JUN 5: Former Vice President Joe Biden surpasses the required 1,991 delegates to win the Democratic nomination

JUN 6: The World Health Organization announces that all people should wear masks in public to help stop the spread of coronavirus

JUN 7: Republican Senator Mitt Romney joins a march with evangelical Christians against racism

JUN 7: The number of worldwide cases of COVID-19 surpasses seven million and with 26% of all cases the US remains the global epicenter

JUN 8: George Floyd's casket is displayed in Houston drawing thousands of mourners. Joe Biden, the Democratic presidential candidate, meets with Floyd's family

JUN 8: Seattle police abandon a precinct located in the Capitol Hill neighborhood. Activists rename the neighborhood the Capitol Hill Occupied Protest (CHOP) area

JUN 10:	NASCAR bans the Confederate flag from racetracks and facilities
JUN 12:	In Atlanta, a Black man, Rayshard Brooks, is killed by a police officer after falling asleep in a Wendy's restaurant drive-through lane
JUN 16:	President Trump signs an executive order limiting the use of police chokeholds except in cases where "deadly force is allowed by law"
JUN 17:	Death toll due to the COVID-19 pandemic in the United States has surpassed the number of American casualties during World War I (Johns Hopkins University)
JUN 18:	In a 5-4 ruling, the Supreme Court blocks the Trump administration's attempt to end DACA (Deferred Action for Childhood Arrivals)
JUN 19:	Lawmakers in Tennessee pass the country's toughest antiabortion laws, banning the procedure from the moment of fetal heartbeat, occurring at around six weeks of pregnancy
JUN 20:	President Trump holds his first rally since the start of the coronavirus pandemic. The rally in Tulsa, Oklahoma, drew about 6,200 people to the BOK Center which seats 19,199
JUN 24:	A Republican bill intended to reform US policing fails in the Senate after civil rights leaders, activist groups and Senate Democrats call it irrevocably flawed
JUN 24:	Leaders of Seattle's Capitol Hill Autonomous Zone announce the zone's disestablishment
JUN 28:	The world surpassed two grim milestones with 500,000 confirmed deaths and 10 million confirmed cases of COVID-19 globally
JUN 28:	Princeton University says it will remove the name of former US President Woodrow Wilson from its public policy school and from a residential college, calling him "a racist"
JUN 30:	China passes a controversial national security bill that allows Chinese officials to operate in Hong Kong and enforce laws regarding secession, subversion against the central Chinese government, terrorist activities, and collusion with foreign forces to endanger national security

Lament

JUNE 1, 2020

SUZANNE TEDESKO

We believed with Obama
change finally had come,
an upward trajectory
toward a more evolved world.

That magical thinking
hid a much darker truth—
white extremists were lurking
like the COVID-19.
When a Black man
gained the grand prize
they met in their covens
and laid out their plans.

As a grandma I grieve
for the mess that we've made,
for the world we are leaving—
so at odds with our dreams.

With our '60's idealism
we thought we could change things,
leave a just world for our children—
that became my North Star;
untethered to religion
it gave my life purpose,
channeled my passage,
coxswained the course.

Today
I feel anguish
for those with Black skin,
outrage at a system
that bolsters injustice
then pretends not to see,
ashamed of my whiteness
embarrassed by my privilege,
and now cooped up by the virus

feeling hopeless and helpless,
wondering

what I can do.

I Cry!

JUNE 3, 2020

WANDA HERNDON

Home alone, I cry.

I cry for my ancestors, stolen from African homes
To suffer injustice of slavery in America
Viewed as human beasts of burden
They died.

I cry for my people who survived this shameful history
Oppressed and terrorized, their tears watered the roots of inequality
They suffered.

I cry for an American dream lost
Replaced by a Black person's nightmare then and now
Only we understand.

I cry for members of my race, callously slain by evil
Ku Klux Klan, vigilantes, neighbors, and the law
Thousands still die.

I cry about poverty and destitution engulfing our communities
Unbreakable cycles of despair begun so long ago on slave ships,
plantations
Few escape.

I cry, incensed by the murder of yet another Black person
Knee on neck, asleep in bed, jogging in their neighborhood
America is our country too.

I cry because we are not welcome
We are tolerated by those who say, "It wasn't me"
A perk of White privilege.

I cry because our sacrifices for America are unrecognized
And our deficiencies emphasized
Equity eludes us.

I cry because our ancestors died for my chance
Decades later, hate still festers and threatens our souls
The pain is too much.

I cry for justice.

From: Mary Ann GONZALES
Subject: Protests
Date: June 12, 2020 at 3:26:13 PM PDT
To: Tyson Greer, Beth Weir, Laura Lippman, Suzie Tedesko, Wanda Herndon, Jane Spalding

I just returned from a Protest. I really was not going downtown. But I got a message from a neighbor that Loyal Heights (the whitest neighborhood in Seattle) was having a protest. I think that maybe the PTA or some such called it. But on 80th street for about three blocks stood families. I thought maybe 300 to 350 bodies. From babes in arms, school kids mostly with signs, a few teenagers that didn't actually know what to do with their long legs, and young parents. Quite likely I was the oldest in attendance. Of course, it rained. But the kids called slogans back and forth across the street, cars honked horns and everyone wore their masks. My heart smiled and it was all I could do not to weep with the possibility that these children will remember. Then maybe they will act. Maybe.

Some Days

JUNE 16, 2020

TYSON GREER

Some days are better than others.

When someone asks me how I feel, like a rat in a lab I push the "I'm fine" button. It's as automatic as breathing. In-out-I'm-fine.

I think Jim and I began isolating early in March... might have been middle of the month. Keeping score doesn't matter.

Winter has passed. What passes for spring is gone. Rhodys have bloomed, gloriously actually, as have the irises, bluebells, tulips, daffodils. The rainbow color is gone, the garden is green, green, green; but the roses are trying, if they're not choked by the white bindweed that clamors up their stalks.

Is it the lack of structure, which I had embraced with such childhood joy? Wheeee—no appointments! No schedule! I'm freeeeeeeeeeeee. Free for what?

I have a list but lack luster to tackle it. I respond to the urgent— Sourdough needs to be fed! Do it tonight before going to bed!—but I place the jar in the fridge, where it can sleep, unfed, unattended, hibernating, waiting.

Waiting for

...what?

Waiting for ...

the news to get better?

Tired of the outrage I see and I feel. Are we there yet? Not by a long shot. Another shot in the dark.

How can anyone on this earth find fault with someone holding a sign: Black Lives Matter? How on this earth can anyone not feel rage at the fact that someone has to hold up a sign, to say it, to sing it, to shout it—to FINALLY have it heard that BLACK LIVES MATTER and accept it as norm? Dark clouds gather, but will they bring a rain of redemption?

When did the puffed-up proud phrase "tell truth to power" slip out of our lexicon? The problem is: power. Power doesn't have to listen and knows it— that's the truth about power. And it has no intention of reconciling.

Waiting for

...the new normal.

When will the act of putting on a mask be as routine as putting on a seat belt? Facebook is suffocating under the weight of people patiently pleading "do it for others." And this has to be explained? What this says about our culture is not worth repeating. Why does a little mask have the power to divide the once-united states of America?

Some days are better than others.

I've had days where I jump out of bed, to go write, to see the sun touch the leaves, to feel the cool grass under bare feet. Days when the writing flowed like the North Fork of the Skykomish—bright and fast—or like the Columbia—steady and sure.

And I've savored time, time to pause. I've felt the warmth of the sun on my shoulder and Jim by my side, savoring the strawberries—we'd picked them that morning—swimming in the warm cinnamoned oatmeal and milk; tasting the crunch of walnut bits and the sweet crispness of fresh cut apples. I watch the lake. On many mirror-still mornings, a lone water skier—our favorite one—inscribes the surface like a skater on ice. Some afternoons, white caps dance with joy.

Even without a dog, we take daily morning walks, side by side, down the middle of quiet streets—moving meditations—no cars, seldom people. Day by day, we watch leaves unfurl and flower buds go from secrets to swelling. Smell the fresh rain. Scan the trees, hope for the high-pitched call of eagles, watch the brazen crows dive at them. Look for the big seal-point Siamese soft-coated cat that rolls on the ground begging for touch on Shore Drive and the skinny young orange cat who trots with us for a while on 41st.

There's the physical pleasure of yanking out winter's weeds, hauling wheelbarrows of mulch over bumpy ground, flinging it under expectant rhododendrons, azaleas, and blueberry bushes, and turning the dark ragged earth into a treasure hunt for juncos and towhees.

And some days, sitting in the green leather chair I've turned toward the big windows, I watch the water, the fish hawks and the hummers, and wait for Mt. Rainier.

Some days are better than others.

So Many Years Ago

JUNE 18, 2020

MARY ANN GONZALES

So many years ago it is hard to remember, Beth Weir and I sat on hard chairs in a writing class in the basement of the Greenwood Senior Center. For reasons we never completely understood the teacher kicked out one of our favorite students. Eventually we gathered him and one other student and invited both men and their wives to dinner. We were a cardiologist, a math teacher, a retired college professor, and a social worker. Since that time we have gathered for dinners, sometimes bringing our writings, but always came away refreshed in our friendships.

When we agreed a virus was interrupting our gatherings, we decided we would not allow that! Beth and Bruce were at the last minute unable to attend, but the rest of us gathered on the shady patio of one of our members. As we sat in our approved six-foot distance, not sharing food from a common plate, it was fun to see that the face masks we all wore were ones that I had sewn for them.

It was a joy to re-connect. We are all quite "long in the tooth" so we had to have a health check in. (The latest cancer scan, does CBD oil help arthritic hands, etc.) Soon we moved on to the more topical issues mostly having to do with our political situation, the trips we were now not taking and the ones we had previously enjoyed. and how difficult isolation is to endure.

This was a quiet, life-giving gathering to connect with valued friends. I suspect gatherings of this type are happening throughout the world. We are but bit players in this sad COVID drama.

Skyschool

JUNE 20, 2020

SUZANNE TEDESKO

The pandemic rages on, police reform legislation has stalled in Congress, two teenagers were shot this morning in the CHOP zone on Capitol Hill, and yet a bright light in the form of a small child is drawing me out of my gloom and teaching me oodles along the way. Since the first of June when our son-in-law returned to work after two months of paternity leave, Bill and I have spent Mondays, Wednesdays and Fridays with our three-year-old grandson.

Our daughter, who works full-time from home while juggling the demands of their four-month-old, pulled Sky out of his Spanish immersion preschool in late February after chatting with a dad picking up his own child. COVID-19 had just erupted in a nursing home on Seattle's Eastside and this dad was an ER doc in the hospital serving those infected. Rather than send Sky back to preschool which remained open to serve children of essential workers, Bill ("Poppie") and I ("Oma") offered to conduct Skyschool. While I've never formally taught young children, I was determined to create a loose structure and engage his curiosity and eagerness with learning activities. To bone up I ordered a couple books with preschool teaching ideas but they never arrived, leaving me to create experiential learning activities on the fly.

Monday, 8:45 am. Each day begins with outdoor exploration. Sky waits on his porch steps with mask, mini-backpack and some tiny item in hand. With playgrounds now closed, we walk in the forest, on the beach or through neighborhoods noting giant trees, Dead End signs and fairy gardens as guideposts. Sometimes we snake through trails at Camp Long on foot, or I sprint to keep up as Sky rides his strider towards a favored destination: the climbing wall where he sets down the strider to clamber up the steep stone rise.

Sky loves flowers. Now on our walks, he remembers both the names of flowers we taught him over a year ago—"Poppie, look at that foxglove," and factoids I may have forgotten: "Don't touch those, Oma." He points to a euphorbia. "They have poison in them."

Ever since infancy Sky has seemingly needed to hold something in his hand at all times, even at night as he's tucked into bed. I figure it's a 21st century version of a 'blankie' since loose bedding for babies is considered hazardous. (Now that he's older, he'll agree to put the object in his pocket if he needs to use both hands.) On a recent walk one sparkly Lincoln Park morning, the object he carried was a tiny mirror. Bill showed him how to catch a ray of light and shine it as a signal. For the rest of the walk, Sky practiced illuminating patches of ground or shooting beams into the canopy of trees. On a similarly bright morning, we notice that tiny daisy-like posies have opened where morning sun breaks through while those in shade still curl up in sleep.

Oftentimes, something we encounter on our walk will suggest an art or craft activity for later in the day. The wing-like seed pods from under a big-leaf maple, 'samaras'—Sky teaches me the word—would make wonderful wings for little creatures. We add forked twigs, peeled strips of bark, cedar berries and clumps of moss to the collection container that I always carry with me now, and that afternoon, make tiny fairy dolls.

When we get back to our house, I ask him to choose a letter-of-the-day. "B, I want B," he says. "OK, B it is." As Bill prepares lunch, I scurry around to gather small objects from around the house—a ball, a bat, a bowl and a bottle, a book, a bird, a basket and a bucket, a banana and a bear, for a scavenger hunt. I make a list numbering the items one through ten with the word and a crude drawing for each, hide them in the front yard and set him loose.

Once after a spate of rain and wind, we deadhead blooms from the red geranium on our porch and notice our hands are purple. Wondering what other blossoms might make natural dyes, we set off through the neighborhood to gather moist, downed petals: purple rhodys, more geraniums, buttercups and dandelions, cornflowers, roses and lithadora. Back at our art table, Sky smooshes them one by one onto thick paper to make a watercolor for his mom.

After lunch it's time for a story. In *Frog and Toad*, the friends make a list and then cross off each completed task. Like Frog and Toad, Sky and I make a list of what we've done so far and Sky crosses each off. Then I add to the list: take a nap, play, have a snack, tend the garden, go home, have dinner, go to bed. When he wakes up, he grabs a pencil and strikes 'take a nap.'

Afternoon playtime. After building a tower, and then, knocking down a dozen plastic cups which I've set in staggered rows for an improvised round of bowling, Sky finds in the toy bin a tiny metal disk. "What's this?" he asks. "It looks like a hubcap that's come off a toy truck." We talk about hubcaps—how some cars have all four, others not but they're not essential for the wheels to work. We go outside to check our cars for missing hubcaps but now he's obsessed: he needs to check each car on the next three blocks, all four wheels, for missing hubcaps. Our walk turns into a hubcap identification and counting exercise. Now I can describe a variety of wheel coverings for Subarus, Hondas, and Jettas. Who knew? Maybe when my preschool teaching days are over, I can become a car mechanic.

The Power of One

JUNE 23, 2020

BETH WEIR

Now we are at four months. The lockdown is well past being novel and the virus continues to obey its awful genetic programing. As of writing it has killed 456,726 persons globally. That figure is only going up.

Since nothing has changed—we still have the unrelenting deaths and infections and no immunity—my particular duty remains confining myself to barracks, so that is what I do. Happily, the oncoming summer provides some license to meet with friends outside where it is safer. In concert with this ongoing personal dislocation, is the widespread and continuing unrest in support of the Black Lives Matter movement. It has authored an earthquake-like shift in the social landscape that is both wrenching and positive. What has vexed me personally is figuring out how I can be part of the solution when I should stay at home. How to leverage my contribution so it could be meaningful?

Enter Carol Anderson, a Black historian at Emory University in Atlanta. She appeared on Zoom, June 21, as part of Seattle's Arts and Lectures Series and spoke for nearly two hours. (As an aside, she never once used a language filler such a um or ah. I take note of such things! I was in awe at her eloquence, not to mention her deep grasp of the issues.)

Anderson's latest book has the provocative name of *One Person: No Vote* and, as the title suggests, is an examination of the history of vote suppression in the US. Anderson made clear for the audience that the laws enacted to close down voting have a veneer of lawfulness that a closer look repudiates. Legislators explain they are adding protections against voter fraud, despite the fact that multiple investigations have not turned up any. While blatant suppression measures such as the poll tax is no more, the ability to vote is still being infringed upon with remarkable dexterity: requiring a physical address to register is one example. It is a near impossibility for Native Americans who live on reservations to cite one. Having the required government ID to vote, designated as all kinds, except those for subsidized housing in which the majorities of residents are Black, is another.

As an original and deep thinker can do, Anderson demonstrated how the seemingly disparate issues surrounding social injustice are interconnected. When asked where people should donate, she suggested any of the known and respected organizations that fight prejudice and its cousins.

The power of one is indeed to be revered. I was enormously grateful to this woman when she finished her talk. She lit up the dim tunnel I'd be patting my way around after the confusion of the past weeks and enabled me to focus. Carol Anderson made me feel that it is time to start something new and to trust the magic of a new beginning.

Freezing the Memories at Four Months

JUNE 27, 2020

BETH WEIR

Every time I try to finish the sentence, "living through the coronavirus is like..."
I come up short. Simply, it has no analog.

The experience itself is easy enough to describe. I stay at home, except for
grocery shopping, doctor appointment or haircuts. But these trips do little
to liberate the spirit since we have to stay in our car till texted, mask up and
then stand at the requisite social distance when discussing what needs to be
discussed. An expression a friend once told me in a too-much-information
moment, applies here. Using a condom is like wearing a sock. It is necessary but
not as satisfying as it could be.

The coronavirus happened to appear at a politically urgent moment in the
United States. Election year politics are unfolding as is President Trump in the
face of the health crisis and his precipitously falling polls. I always thought the
man was ridiculous, but his cornbread is truly not baked in the middle any-
more as we close in to 100 days from the election. He proclaimed to a sea of red
MAGA hats at a political rally, and I paraphrase, that testing for the coronavirus is not a good idea because it means we discover more cases. In addition,
the Black Lives Matter movement has gained traction unimagined before the
murder of George Floyd. It has led the nation into necessary and protracted
soul searching.

In our personal situation we are saddened by the fact that currently two
friends, one of which has been so for over fifty years, are in hospice.

But, the human spirit being what it is, there are moments in this life being
lived simultaneously in a big and a little fashion, that bring joy. Or something
of note. They tend to appear serendipitously.

On my walks with our terrier, Jack I see kids out riding unicycles and they
are anxious to show off their skills. "Want to see me go backwards?" one little
boy asked. "Want to see how fast I can go?" a pink-cheeked girl, pigtails flying,
offered as she whizzed down the empty street. Kids on bikes feels good.

I have a garden that is currently feeding us—beets, lettuce, peas, Swiss
chard, and the crème de la crème, fava beans. The latter are impossible to
purchase. They are also an easy way to my husband's heart. We have picked
currants, rhubarb and soon we will have new potatoes to pair with our mint
supply.

Having a garden sort of makes up for my rather odd sourdough bread loaves
baked when there was no yeast available. It took a while to get the hang of making starter and when I finally did it grew like Audrey, the plant in Little Shop of
Horrors. All. Over. My. Kitchen. Kudos to my friend Tyson who rescued me.

The heated objections of some individuals to wearing masks has me scratching my head. They refuse in the name of freedom. Didn't their mothers ever explain that you pick your hill to die on and this one is barely a mound?

Along with normally well-coiffed friends, we slide into sloth across Zoom sessions. Gone is make up and blow-dried hair. Personally, I have learned how to give haircuts. Bruce is easy, just a question of zipping the razor over his head. I find his bald spot a bit of a challenge and often have a stray hair wave at me when done. Jack, the dog, is slightly more challenging and has the canine equivalent of a bowl cut, but he holds no grudges.

Some things are no fun at all. Watching the dates for planned trips come and go—as in New Zealand and New York—has been hard. It is made harder by the fact we have no idea when we can get traveling again.

Some events are unique but have resonance because of the times. Sharing gin and tonic at 11:30 one Friday morning with a neighbor over the fence, the day I sent off a novel to an agent was a high note, and something I'm unlikely to repeat. Nor am I likely to be asked as a character reference for an adoption of a baby again.

And some things are plain mysterious. Because I don't have much on my calendar, I usually double book when I do. That is one of the mysteries of the times. As are the photos I intended to digitize. They are still in the box where I left them at the start of the pandemic. Maybe in the next four months!

COVID Connection

JUNE 30, 2020

TYSON GREER

Today, as is typical in Seattle,
is foggy and cool—
57 degrees:
Is it June?
Or is it January?
My watch says it's June 30th, the last day of June.

At my desk, I'm grateful for the view
of the mist-subdued hills across the lake
and the swath of spunky white daisies in my upper garden
and the new green rhody leaves lifting their palms in prayer—
pray, when will we stop combining
the word "social"
with the word "distance"?

Last Friday,
a spectacularly sunny day,
Jim and I had our first backyard "social":
lunch with four of us
sitting separately—
or rather, two on blue canvas director chairs

      with   a   great   gulf   of   blue-painted   patio

between us and
the other two on a bench.
Separate seating, separate tables.

According to the rules of the game
we four had lunch "together."
They brought theirs
we ferried ours downstairs.
They brought their coffee
we sipped our iced tea.

After lunch
we encouraged them to graze

the raspberry bushes.
An in-home "You Pick" is the height
of in-hospitality.

But still, we were glad
for this summer's version of
"together."

Together—laughing, trading stories,
catching up on the grandkids,
what-are-you-reading—
where any pause in the conversation is
companionable.

Unlike Zoom, where even several seconds
of "dead air,"
staring at little rectangles of each other,
you rush to fill the air-space
for fear you'll lose
connection.

Connection, to me,
is the essence of humanness.

So today, from my desk, I look out
at the swath of daisies nodding companionably,
and to the two empty director's chairs
and the empty wood bench.

The card table is bare,
the old blue and white cloth taken upstairs.
The view brings a smile
because the feeling remains—
even on the chilly last day of June—
of a day warm with friendship
        and
of being connected.

JULY 2020

JUL 1:   Europe opens its borders to 15 safe countries after months of lockdown, excludes the US, Brazil and Russia

JUL 1:   US confirms more than 50,000 new COVID-19 cases in one day for the first time

JUL 1:   Texas Governor Greg Abbott makes wearing face masks mandatory as cases of COVID-19 soar in the state

JUL 5:   Florida reports a record 11,458 daily COVID-19 cases

JUL 6:   US officially begins withdrawing from WHO

JUL 7:   Texas records more than 10,000 daily cases of COVID-19 for the first time

JUL 8:   US government issues directive that more than 1 million international students will be stripped of their visas if their courses are entirely online

JUL 19:   Portland Mayor Ted Wheeler criticizes federal policing of protesters in his city, calling it unconstitutional

JUL 22:   California passes New York total for COVID-19 cases (415,763 vs 415,094), though NY death toll much higher

JUL 23:   US confirms COVID-19 cases pass 4 million with death toll over 143,000. Real number of cases likely up to 13x higher (CDC)

JUL 24:   President Trump says he could send 75,000 federal agents to deal with violence in American cities like Portland, drawing backlash

JUL 25:   Hurricane Hanna, first of the 2020 season, makes landfall on the Texas Gulf Coast as a Category 1 storm

JUL 26:   US Congressman John Lewis becomes the first Black lawmaker to lie in state in the Rotunda in Washington D.C.

JUL 27:   Google decides its employees can work from home until July 2021, the largest tech company to commit to working from home

JUL 28: WHO head Tedros Adhanom Ghebreyesus states that COVID-19 is "easily the most severe" global health emergency the WHO has faced

JUL 30: Barack Obama gives the eulogy at the funeral of Congressman John Lewis, with former presidents George W. Bush and Bill Clinton at Ebenezer Baptist Church in Atlanta

JUL 30: US economy posts the largest quarterly fall on record with GDP down 9.5% for the 3 months to June 30

JUL 30: Federal law enforcement officers begin a phased withdrawal from Portland amid criticism of their actions to shut down Black Lives Matter protests

JUL 30: Apple Wildfire starts near Beaumont, California, forcing the evacuation of nearly 8,000 people over the next few days

How Do I Talk to My Sister?

JULY 2, 2020

TYSON GREER

My sister, older by two years, lives in the lovely town of Beaufort, South Carolina. I found home (after experimenting with several states) in the lovely town of Lake Forest Park, Washington. We are separated by distance but care deeply for each other.

I wonder, since she's white and living in the South, how would she feel if someone called her a "cracker"? Would she feel insulted? Or would she shrug it off? No one has put a knee on her neck.

Say their names:

George Floyd

Breonna Taylor

Rayshard Brooks

Atatiana Jefferson

Aura Rosser

Stephon Clark

I remember reading that people can't remember more than seven items in a list.

Botham Jean

Philando Castille

Alton Sterling

Michelle Cusseaux

Freddie Gray

Freddie Gray. My sister and I spent our early childhood in a tidy Baltimore rowhouse up the street from WBAL-TV where Oprah got her start. When my sister was eleven and I was nine, our family moved to the white-burbs. We share blonde hair, blue eyes, a love of gardening and cooking, and we are sometimes a continent apart in our views.

Recently, my sister told me, "More police officers are shot and killed by Blacks than police officers kill African-Americans."

I admit data is murky: some agencies don't report, different departments record data differently. Is it "shootings" only, or taser-deaths, beating deaths, chokehold-deaths, or knee-on-neck deaths?

Say their names:

Janisha Fonville

Eric Garner

Akai Gurley

Gabriella Nevarez

"What do you think about the Black people killing police?" my sister asked. I agreed killing was wrong.

In 2019, 48 police officers were killed as a result of felonious acts, e.g., 13 during criminal investigations, 9 in tactical situations, 5 in unprovoked attacks, 4 during crimes in progress, and so on. (FBI Uniform Crime Reporting Program)

In the same year, of the 1002 deaths at the hands of law enforcement, 250 (25%) were Black, yet Blacks make up only 13% of the US population. (*The Washington Post*)

Say their names out loud:

Tamir Rice

Michael Brown

Tanisha Anderson

Black men and boys risk death by police at the rate of 96 out of 100,000; white men and boys, 39 out of 100,000. (Proceedings of the National Academies of Sciences Study, 2019)

My sister is a good person. Once a week she reads stories to a preschool class of predominantly Black children. But the problem with my sister and me is more than inhabiting separate coasts, it's that we inhabit worlds defined by different truths and separate views of reality.

Jacob Blake

Trayvon Martin...

Do the math.
8 minutes, 46 seconds.
I feel my chest tighten. So many names to say.

Hospice House

JULY 4, 2020

JANE SPALDING
Tacoma, Washington

"We are still knee-deep in the first wave of this," says Dr. Anthony Fauci in today's news. Ten thousand cases in one day in Florida. A steady climb in the number of new cases in Washington. From a consistent level in the low 200's to yesterday's report of 1,087. What's a body to do? Choose who's in your bubble very carefully.

One person in my bubble is Sherry Schultz, my longtime friend who is the Director of Volunteer Services at CHI Franciscan Hospice, one of the largest hospice centers in the country. The mission of hospice is to offer comprehensive end-of-life care to patients and their families throughout King, Kitsap and Pierce counties. Since 1990, when I introduced Sherry to the Director of Hospice in Snohomish County, she has been involved in one way or another in hospice work. First as a director of development, then as a chaplain and now she manages a robust volunteer program. At least it used to be robust.

These days volunteers are not permitted to work in the 20-bed inpatient Hospice House, or to visit the 700+ patients who receive care in their homes. Sherry and her staff of six are scrambling to maintain a minimum level of the services once provided by the more than 200 volunteers. That means they do such things as staff the front desk, offer educational programs via Zoom in an effort to keep volunteers engaged, and deliver flowers.

July 3 was Sherry's last Friday off due to a budget shortfall. The good news is she is going back to work full time this week. She and I arranged to spend Friday and Saturday together in Tacoma. Shortly after I arrived, she got a call from a member of her staff who retrieves slightly-past-their-prime-flowers on Wednesday and Friday from Trader Joe's, delivers them to Hospice House, and arranges and distributes them. She wasn't going to be able to do it. Sherry assured her it was okay and encouraged her to enjoy the day off.

Then she said to me, "I need to go pick up the flowers, but you don't have to."

"No, no, I want to come," I said, pleased to have a reason to go someplace after months of being housebound.

By about 6 pm, we arrived at Trader Joe's. Even though this transaction happens twice a week, the TJ's staff member was very enthusiastic about donating flowers and plants to Hospice House. He had eight huge boxes filled and ready to load into Sherry's Toyota Corolla. Well that wasn't going to work. So, we consolidated, mashing roses and alstroemeria on top of carnations, tulips, and sunflowers. One whole box was filled with rosemary plants and other assorted things in pots.

"You don't have to take everything," the store employee said. "I'm not sure why we have so many today." Then he opened another box and gushed over the roses. "Oh, look at these orange ones. They're so pretty with the purple ones." His obvious pleasure in what he was doing provided a bright spot amidst an ongoing stream of bad news.

We managed to take every bloom and plant and deliver them all to Hospice House, where we clipped the stems, and left them in buckets of water with plans to come back the next day to arrange and distribute.

As a friend of Sherry's, I felt privileged to be allowed to enter Hospice House. Visitors are limited to two family members at a time and no volunteer can come in. Just inside the door is a hand sanitizing station, then comes donning a surgical mask, followed by a temperature check. Sherry put a wand-like thermometer into a plastic bag, touched my forehead twice and behind my ear once and said "98.6, welcome to Hospice House. Please take a visitor nametag."

In the cramped quarters of the volunteer office we arranged hundreds of flowers, which Sherry distributed throughout the building. We also offered a bouquet to the occasional staff member who walked by. "Roses? What color would you like?" And a "Thank you for what you do," perhaps brightening the day of a nurse working a holiday weekend.

We were down to the last ten or twelve bundles when I picked up a beautiful bouquet of two dozen white tulips and said, "These are gorgeous and they're not going to last very long. Can't we give them to someone to take home?"

Sherry's solution was to fill two buckets with water and the remaining bouquets and put one in the staff room and one at the front desk. Before we left, the person working the front desk stopped by to tell us she had just given a bouquet to a sad visitor. "It was great to see her smile," she reported.

The flowers survived their dodgy donated life. Spared from a massive recycling bin, they found new purpose by adding a touch of beauty to ease others' lives.

Because of some COVID-related regulation, flowers can no longer go into patient rooms. And lilies can't go anywhere. So, I'm admiring a gorgeous display of white and deep purple lilies gracing my kitchen table, remembering the gracious staff we encountered, and feeling humbled.

COVID Date: March 126th, 2020

JULY 4, 2020

TYSON GREER

According to my calendar, which this year looks more like the Arctic tundra than a busy bunch of bees, it's July 4, 2020. But it feels like we are frozen in time—it feels as if March has gone on forever—and space. Especially space. My compass needle drifts, trying to hold on to thingsthatmatter.

We're very familiar with our space. Living room, bedroom, kitchen. Rinse and repeat. Back garden, deck, front garden. Rinse and repeat.

Blueberries are unusually early this year... That's been good. Typically, we struggle to get six by the 4th for our patriotic red (raspberries), white (vanilla ice cream), and blue (berries) celebration on the deck with friends, oohing and ahh-ing at the Sheridan Beach pyrotechnic display (and worrying about "Where do the eagles and osprey go when Sheridan Beach imitates the rocket's red glare?"). But no big fireworks this year.

Alone on July 4th, we did wave at our neighbors, Cynthia and Roger, on their deck. Professional pyrotechnic displays were down, fireworks sales were up, as evidenced by the rockets from neighbors and all around the lake. But the full moon rising over the hills across the lake was the most spectacular display of all. Quieter too.

Separated by distance, Jim and I called the "boys"—Erik in Woodinville, James in Warm Springs, John in Gallup, Jeff in Auburn, Aaron in L.A. Long talks and laughter eased the emptiness of distance.

And we ate. For breakfast, I got out the flag-themed placemats on top of the blue and white Ukrainian tablecloth and found the red and white check-ered napkins (the red squares were actually little red crabs with a nod to my Baltimore blue crab heritage).

Topped the table off with a flower arrangement of white daisies and red cro-cosmias blooming out of a royal blue rectangular glass vase. Quite a festive set-ting for the bacon and buckwheat pancakes—the carrier vehicles for our own fresh-picked raspberries and blueberries that have bloomed in such abundance.

But not feeling very patriotic. The shame of a president presiding over Mount Rushmore demanding fireworks over sacred ground and spewing lies over his mask-less worshippers. COVID deaths climb and the president blasphemes protest-ers who raise their voices that Black Lives Matter. This doesn't feel like my country.

Powerlessness grips me. What can I do to soothe generations of racial pain and turn the tide from racial abuse—conscious or unconscious—to empathy and acceptance? What can I do to change minds? To getoutthevote?

Fear haunts me. And what if in November, the country votes him out and he refuses to leave? What if he rages and disavows the election—"voter fraud," a banner he's already waving—and insists on an investigation before he turns over the country...and the Republican Senators back him. No ceremony on a cold January day, or on a chilling February day...something that should be unthinkable... he's still there?

So, I make another flower arrangement—red, white, and blue—and remember when the date felt like something to be proud of. We watch the *Hamilton* musical, hoping to rev up a little historic patriotism. Liked the music, but dueling is stupid and wasn't Hamilton a slave owner?

How do I figure out what the hell I can do that would matter?

The day after the 4th, we visit our Woodinville family. We sit outside with the 13-year-old boys, inhaling their presence—from a safe distance of 10-12 feet—and abide in an oasis of caring, love, and thingsthatmatter. I've missed them so much, it's almost a physical ache. And I ache for my own mother enduring decades of distance between Baltimore and Philadelphia-New Mexico-New York-Nevada-Europe-Seattle—all the places I've lived with my sons, and she so far from her grandsons. Different shades of distance.

We sit and chat. One of our grandsons started strength-training in January, before COVID-time. He explains the exercises he's doing now and the progress he's making. The other grandson recounts data on the darkness of transmission—receiving or giving—the percentages and the rising curve, and on persistent racism and gender-based intolerance that degrades these "States," no longer so "United." What can I say to comfort? I can listen and hear. Both boys are sensitive and intelligent, and I'm greedy to know what they think and feel, especially since March 1. Still, it's hard knowing that they know things that shouldn't burden 13-year-olds. But this is COVID-time.

Erik and Luia come home from errands and, after a bit, the boys drift away and we four adults banter and catch up—Garden's looking great. How's work? How's isolation? When do you go back? Thanks for the bamboo poles for the pea vines. Have you watched *Hamilton*?

When we leave—it's almost seven, hard to tell on a sunny July day—I feel giddy with joy. I don't feel more patriotic, but I feel satisfied, buoyed, and reconnected with thingsthatmatter. It's all I can do for this day.

Speak!

JULY 15, 2020

WANDA HERNDON

Beyond US borders
Distant friends declare
that I speak American, not English.
It's news to me.

We discuss, debate, laugh, and chat
Encourage, support, relax.
They listen to words flowing over my lips,
with a distinct accent.

Skeptics raise eyebrows when
they hear me speak
in powerful sentences
with noun-verb agreement.

Clear and coherent
What do they expect?
Ebonics, a valid Black language,
that I also speak.

It's a punch in my gut,
for every Black person alive,
when articulate and well-spoken
are used to describe.

A compliment composed of these words
Make my ears burn
It's obvious they are oblivious.
Dose the fire, breathe, move on.

Our dialects may be different,
our experiences unique.
American is my first language.

Listen when I speak.

A Schedule and a Garden

JULY 16, 2020

BETH WEIR

If my generally optimistic mother ever talked about raising two children by herself during the Second World War, it was to tell me there was no end to her day. My father, then in Egypt, never came home to 'start' the evening. Time blurred, grew wavy and inconsiderate.

During the pandemic, I have begun to understand why my mother reported this experience. I am retired, in the susceptible age group and so can best contribute to the coronavirus fight by staying out of harm's way. At the time of writing I have been home for nearly four months and have discovered my mother's truth about the need for contours to a day.

My personal circumstance is positive so I have the advantage of the 'deluxe' version of sacrifice. My still working spouse has a schedule that gives structure to mealtimes, while the dog, oblivious to anything but his own needs, requires his daily walk. Preferably at 11 am when he is ready for one after his morning nap. Each morning I tidy up the most egregious messes in the house, do a spot of writing and after lunch dive into the garden. It is not so strict an observance that I cannot pop in periodically to Bruce's office to chat. He brings me coffee at 10 and tea at 2 or thereabouts.

Still, even a careful hewing to a schedule cannot save me, or any sentient being I would venture, from the roller-coaster emotions of the moment. The daily serving of distressing news about the ravages of COVID-19 and the Black Lives Matter protests is shattering.

What I did not anticipate, though, is the effect of personal loss in such times when emotions are already raw. On Sunday morning I woke to a text from a good friend in North Carolina that read Call me ASAP.

"What's happened?" I asked, barely able to breathe.

Ellen burst into tears when she heard my voice. "It's Jane," she said, referring to a mutual friend with whom I once worked and remained close. Together Ellen and I had tracked her progress last year in fighting multiple myeloma. We thought she had licked it, particularly as Ellen reported Jane as perky in a recent get together. "Her curly hair is back after the chemo, as pretty as it ever was." Now Ellen told me on the call, "the cancer has migrated into her brain and lungs. She complains of being tired and is disoriented. It is not good. The family wants privacy."

When I got off the phone I could not determine for whom I was crying. Certainly it was for Jane's seemingly inevitable passing but it was also over the fact that our oldest friend in the US is dying as well. His kidneys are giving up. The list of those close to us who have passed before them across the season of the virus is overlong: a buff, fit graduate school friend, my niece's husband, a former, prickly coworker I was fond of, and she of me, an English friend. None died of COVID-19.

After hearing about my tiny buddy, Jane, all the collective emotions welled up since there is nowhere sturdy to put them right now. Quite apart from the absence of hugs and the funerals that provide solace, there is the generalized agony of the moment. Everyone is hurting.

I did what I generally do when I need to reset my emotional clock—I disappeared into the garden that Sunday afternoon after hearing about Jane. I transferred the compost from two bins into the new raised bed Bruce had built, followed by commercial topsoil and planted leeks, beets, beans and more, with lupins for the bees. The structure of my routine in combination with my affection for gardening was soothing. I did think, though, that I will never again look at a lupin without thinking of Jane.

At one o'clock I heard a robust sound from the neighbor's glossy back garden. That morning it had been set up with a chuppah and white chairs for twenty people. The guests came in masks. The weather had been dreary and rain threatened but the skies cleared into sunshine before the bride walked across the rose petals on the lawn. Her gown was cream, her train long and her groom was smiling like a fool. When he stomped on the wrapped glass and the guests called out "mazel tov," the new marriage covenant was sealed.

I felt a measure of peace as I peered over the fence from my hiding place at the joyous activities. There was the undeniable delight of the moment but the sense of normalcy, even despite the masks, was inordinately welcome.

As I looked about the garden and wondered how I could grieve for my friends, the thought arrived unbidden and welcome. When someone dies I generally bring the grieving partner a plant. I looked about and decided upon a recently planted bush or a tree that reminded me of each of the deceased in my new garden and gave it their name. I would give their living memory to myself. It is the best I can do for the moment.

In the meantime I had my schedule to adhere to and was grateful for that.

She Doesn't Want to

JULY 21, 2020

JANE SPALDING

"She doesn't want to," the email clearly said. Damn! Once again somebody "doesn't want to" do what I am so sure is the right thing.

This time the one who didn't want to was Lady Anastasia, my lovely goldendoodle. Lady A is a people magnet. Little kids come up and ask, "Can I pet your dog?" She's an instant conversation starter among dog lovers. Adorable, gentle, mellow. A perfect dog to visit sick people, patients in hospice care, people in senior residences, right? My friend Sherry, who works for the largest hospice care center in Pierce County promised me she could keep me as busy as I wanted to be if Lady A and I became a pet therapy team. Sounded like a perfect new venture for recently retired me. So, off we went for a four-hour introductory session near the end of 2019 sponsored by Project Canine Therapy Dogs, the organization that provides therapy dog training and certification. Six other hopeful therapy dogs and their owners joined us.

Lady A's manners aren't the best, so we had a crash course on such commands as "leave it," "down with a stay," and "walk with me." When it came time for each dog to walk through a practice test in anticipation of taking the real certification test, Lady A did everything beautifully. The evaluator even said "perfect" as she responded to commands. Next we would each receive an email inviting us to take the certification test or explaining why not. I left the session smugly confident that my dog and I would be the best therapy team ever.

Then came the email:

Hi Jane,

Thank you for attending therapy dog class with Lady Anastasia. It was great to meet both of you. You are welcome to move forward to the exam step with the following notes:

Lady is a very sweet and lovely dog, but we weren't sure if this is something she really wants to do? When she engaged with you, we saw a happy, warm connection. When Missy interacted with her during the practice exam, she "froze up"...we didn't see the happy, relaxed dog we saw engaging with you. It may be that Lady is a dog who just really loves her person. Or maybe she was a bit overwhelmed by the class. We ask that you think about what her typical reactions are when she meets complete strangers or is in strange situations. If it's the response we saw in class, we would say she doesn't want to do this. While she appeared very "calm," what she was really doing was being tolerant and compliant, but she wasn't enjoying it. If you would like to test with her just know that we will be looking for her to be more relaxed and engaged than she was during class.

She doesn't want to? But she's a perfect therapy dog I shouted at the email. What do you mean she doesn't want to? Surely, I can make her be "more relaxed and engaged." And then, sadly, my image of the two of us spreading comfort and good cheer among the sick faded away as I accepted that they were just being honest. Foiled again in my attempt to force what is right according to me.

Now pet therapy teams are a thing of life as we knew it. But what a gift a "dog who just really loves her person" is in a pandemic. From forced isolation I rant to Lady A as our president sends federal troops into cities to "control" demonstrations. And we cheer on people who stand up for Black Lives Matter and encourage everyone to vote.

Living with an upended illusion of control brings some important life lessons front and center: Love generously. The only person I can change is myself. Live one day at a time. Today I chose to go a yoga class on Zoom. I set it up outside, on the deck facing a grove of old growth trees. Lady A slept in a corner on the deck rousing herself to join me in an occasional downward facing dog. A dog who just loves her person. And me, a person who just loves her dog.

Endless Time

JULY 21, 2020

TYSON GREER

A week or two ago—COVID time is slippery—Governor Inslee announced "the 100th day of lockdown." One hundred days feels like One Hundred Years of Solitude.

A month is 30 days, or 31, or this year 29 (Leap Day, the day of the big annual Lake Forest Park Stewardship Foundation Fundraiser and the last time we got together with friends). "One hundred days." Less than half a year for sure, but we don't measure time in base-ten, so it's odd and unfamiliar, which is exactly what our situation is: odd and unfamiliar.

The first few weeks were energizing: TIME TO CLEAN THE BASEMENT! Calling it an "archeological dig" gave it a grand sense of purpose, which matched the scale of the endeavor.

Every day, with enough energy for all seven of the seven dwarfs, the two of us attacked the basement. One growing pile for St. Vincent, another for just-plain-junk, and another for recycling (oh, the trees that died for our papers, but I don't think you'll miss reading one hundred magazine articles authored by Tyson Greer). On trash day, we asked for and were granted space in several of our neighbor's recycling and garbage bins.

In the basement, I eyed six cardboard file boxes. If we had time—which is ironic, we have lots of time—we would have strolled through the six boxes of magazines Jim had lovingly curated in the mid-1970s.

Jim had operated on the assumption that his kids or grandkids would someday be so pleased to find this treasure trove: 1970s *Life*, *Esquire*, *Time* ("They put so much effort into every issue every week, I couldn't throw them away"—as a writer, I can't help but love him for that), *Rolling Stone,* and *National Geographic* (tell me someone who hasn't wondered how to divest themselves of the *Nat Geo* mags in their basement). And the full page, beautifully illustrated Sunday comics of "Prince Valiant." One morning of a sleep-over a few years ago (who's counting?), the grand-twins politely perused the colorful comics and politely declined to take them home.

We do have lots of time. Time now to think, to reflect on how we spend our time.

Time without teasing (or being teased by) the 13-year-old grandsons is one of the hardest facts of isolation. It's missing not only the overnights; or sharing suppers out, bus downtown, plays or movies, and gingerbread; or cheering basketball, track, baseball, or touch football games—it's missing how they went from a tad taller than I (standing very straight almost 5' 4"), to almost as tall as their 5' 8" mother. That's a gap that can never be filled.

Jim and I've designated our four o'clock teatime each day as the time to make-a-pot-of-tea-and-call-a-friend, near or far, to hear their stories, catch up on how they're coping and what they've discovered. In the mornings, rain or shine, we walk the neighborhood, and neighbors and people we've never seen before wave and call out cheery greetings.

I've always said we are blessed with good neighbors. Being separated has brought us closer. Our neighborhood is experiencing a flurry of kindnesses: like serving as my personal Sourdough Starter Support hot line (answering care & feeding questions).

Neighbors shared tomato starts and seedlings (cucumber, lettuce, and bok choi). The jury's still out on whether or not leaving zucchini seedlings on a doorstep is an act of kindness, but the surprise little bags of cookies, scones, and fresh home-grown lettuce definitely are. I'd never imagined what fun it would be to see neighbors' eyes light up when I brought around big bouquets of white flowering plum branches from the dwarf trees I had pruned.

One of the greatest gifts proved it is better to give than receive. Our neighbor to the south, Roger, a Rolling Stones fan, happily received one box, in good condition, of 1975 *Rolling Stone* magazines. He said he had time to read them.

So, if you're interested in a box of *Life* or *Time*...

Animals in the Time of the Coronavirus

JULY 26, 2020

BETH WEIR

The headline about monkeys, revered in Lopburi, Thailand caught my eye. An article that wasn't about COVID, I cheered. Alas, it was not to be. Apparently the macques, who once lived in harmony with the natives in the temples, have had their numbers boosted by tourism to about 8,400 across a few city blocks. These monkeys are known as crab eaters but the visitors bring items more to their liking—coconut yoghurt and strawberry soda are particular favorites. Now that the tourists have been whisked away by the virus, the animals are confused, hungry, and immensely aggressive. (I can relate.) Bring in a truck with fruit for market and the rascals strip it with nary a bare thank you. The trouble is that in a Buddhist-majority culture where culling the creatures would disturb sensibilities, there are few options outside of sterilization for dealing with them. Apparently they rip up buildings and rooms with the zeal of drug-fueled musicians, so they test their unique status frequently.

The closest, but imperfect parallel we have in Seattle right now are rabbits—at least in my neighborhood. Every time my terrier, Jack and I walk we spot three or four at the very least. Like all gardeners I know there are way more. Every sweet leaf that breaks the surface has been mowed down as mercilessly as a chainsaw dismembers a branch. My vegetables have been spared early harvesting only because they are grown in beds too high for the critters to reach. Like the monkeys, the rabbits are emboldened by the fact that dogs are all bluster and no bite when they run after them. In fact, the rabbits sit up on their haunches and turn their brown doe eyes on Jack and me in a game of dare. At least they don't chew my hoses, as do monkeys. Yet.

Strangely, I've had two other encounters with wildlife this week, which is why the monkey headline took my interest. Early Tuesday morning when dressing, I flicked a look outside my bedroom window. Directly in my line of sight was the fattest raccoon on the planet, climbing the fence with the ease of a gymnast. His long claws folded over the top of the fence, one quick pull, over, turn right and off to tackle the neighbor's fence. He looked as comfortable as a college student home with laundry. Aside from worrying if he'd come back for Jack, it was a delightful serendipity.

It was the second of the two meetings with critters that set me alight. Early the following day I opened a side window next to the kitchen counter to catch the through breezes. Later, I went to make tea and was distracted by a rustle of plastic, then a blasting noise. I caught a quick glimpse of a squirrel and then his flashy tail exiting through the hole in the screen he had chewed as a service to himself. He had been after a loaf of homemade bread ensconced in a plastic bag. It was my first encounter with a truly ballsy squirrel and I immediately had some sympathy for the Thais dealing with their monkeys.

In the meantime, Jack the dog sticks rigidly to his routines: eat, nap, lick my toes, walk, play ball, eat, bark at the mailman, inspect the garden, pee for a treat rewarding his tour of duty, then bed. Occasionally it all gets a bit much and he digs a hole and buries his ball. Sigh. At least he is predictable and isn't chewing hoses too. Yet.

COVID-crazy

JULY 27, 2020

WANDA HERNDON

Some of my friends are going "COVID-crazy." They say they are bored, a bit lost, sleeping all the time and their creative energy levels are low. Not me. I am feeling more energetic and creative than I have felt in years. Maybe it is my socially distanced walks with friends that earn me 10,000 steps daily or my twice-a-week private Zoom weight training sessions that are keeping me pumped. Anyway, I am happy to be alive and in good health.

Since I am not running hither and yonder, I am taking time to think about a myriad of situations. I have hours to consider the state of our world and how I can move from outrage to action. When I feel light, I can binge watch entertaining and interesting shows on every streaming network I have added to my already expensive viewing habit, or I can just relax in my comfortable home. However, I do miss physically spending time with friends, and am eager to look into their faces, maskless, and hug them when it is safe again.

I have not spent this much time at home with myself in years, and I like it. Do not get it twisted...I am not saying that I want to be on COVID lockdown forever. Until we're 100% released back into the world, I plan to continue to find joy in the small things that keep me busy like completing my never-ending memoir, expressing emotions through my resurrected love of poetry, shopping in my jam-packed closets instead of retail stores (saving me tons of money), decluttering kitchen cabinets, tossing expired spices, cooking new recipes, re-arranging furniture, sitting on my patio doing absolutely nothing, considering a condo refresh, and writing endless grocery lists that I take with me during senior hours or any hour that suits me.

Even though masks are hot and a bit uncomfortable, wearing them is a small inconvenience for saving my life and the lives of others. So, I will continue to wear them and try to move through this treacherous period without losing my plain and designer statement coverings.

If the only problems facing me are which mask to wear with my daily workout clothes, or the grocery delivery service failed to drop off what was on my list, or yeast was out of stock at every store I visited in the Greater Seattle area, then I say I am pretty darn lucky. And I am grateful that I am only hooked up to my refrigerator and tethered to my cell phone and television, all beasts that need to be fed (in my mind).

Yes, I am fortunate, but I know there are people who are struggling. I pray for their well-being. I pray that those in need will receive assistance from our government, social services and us, their fellow human beings. I sincerely believe we can survive this trauma if we help each other and do not go COVID crazy!

Sleepless in Seattle

JULY 29, 2020

MARY ANN GONZALES

I am generally a champion sleeper, but tonight I am watching the hours crawl by. Usually I snuggle down, pull the covers over and wake up 8 or 9 hours later. Eventually, I realized as I lay in bed, I wasn't going to sleep so I read the posts about the politics and the pandemic. It was the pandemic that was keeping me awake.

It occurred to me that in a couple of weeks I would be 83 years old, a prime suspect for a quick death. Now, I am not afraid of dying, it comes to us all. But, I imagined that since I was in good health, I had some good years left. Now, after nearly five months of pandemic, it floated into my now wide-awake brain that I am right in the bull's eye age population for COVID. Sometimes I am so slow on the uptick.

My family and I have been slouching toward putting my assets in a Trust, so that at my death, my estate would not be bothered by probate issues. Maybe I need to get that conversation on a front burner.

As I lay in bed, my mind wandered around the rooms of my home, imagining the mess my children would be left with if I became infected with this virus, landed in the hospital and died without cleaning out some of my crowded closets or the bureau drawers stuffed full of trinkets from bygone years. Maybe I should finish the book I am writing so it does not join the other manuscripts I have never finished. Would I ever consider giving away any of my books? Or scarves?

Well, now it 3 AM, it is tomorrow. I am going to pick up that book I have been slogging through, it usually puts me to sleep. I can reconsider the legal-emotional issues after breakfast, if I don't put my head back in the sand.

AUGUST 2020

AUG 3: Hurricane Isaias makes landfall in the US as a Category 1 hurricane near Ocean Isle Beach, North Carolina

AUG 4: UN says COVID-19 pandemic has created biggest educational disruption in history affecting nearly 1.6 million students in 190 countries, 94% worldwide

AUG 4: Huge explosions at the port of Beirut, Lebanon, kill more than 200 and leave over 6,000 thousand people injured

AUG 6: COVID-19 detected cases in Africa pass 1 million with 21,983 deaths

AUG 6: US COVID-19 death toll could reach 300,000 by December 1; 70,000 lives saved if masks worn consistently, according to University of Washington study

AUG 9: New Zealand marks 100 days without transmission of COVID-19

AUG 10: Global COVID-19 cases pass 20 million and is accelerating; first 10 million took almost 6 months, second 10 million took just 43 days (Reuters)

AUG 10: Rare windstorm (derecho) hits the US Midwest flattening cornfields, leaving hundreds of thousands without electricity, killing two people

AUG 11: US Democratic candidate for President Joe Biden announces California Senator Kemala Harris is his running mate, the first woman of color selected by a major party

AUG 12: Europe fights a new COVID-19 surge with Germany, France and Spain posting their largest daily infection totals for three months

AUG 17: University of North Carolina at Chapel Hill is the first US college to send students home for the fall semester and convert to online classes after 135 COVID-19 cases detected

AUG 18: Joe Biden is formally nominated as the Democratic party's presidential candidate during the second night of their first ever virtual convention

AUG 18:	California Governor Gavin Newsom declares state of emergency as 27 fires burn across the state amid a continuing heat wave
AUG 19:	Apple becomes the first US company to be valued at $2 trillion, just two years after it reached $1 trillion valuation
AUG 20:	Kamala Harris accepts her nomination for vice president, becoming the first US woman of color on a major-party ticket, saying "there is no vaccine for racism"
AUG 22:	Fires burning in Northern California declared Major Disaster with LNU Lightning Complex Fire (341,243 acres) and SCU Lightning Complex Fire (339,968) among the three largest wildfires in state history
AUG 22:	Mexican COVID-19 death toll passes 60,000, world's third highest
AUG 23:	US Republican Party Convention begins by formally renominating Donald Trump for a second presidential term
AUG 23:	Jacob Blake is shot and injured by police in front of his children in Kenosha, Wisconsin, prompting violent protests
AUG 27:	Australian terrorist Brenton Tarrant sentenced to life without parole, for the killing of 51 mosque worshippers in Christchurch, New Zealand
AUG 27:	Hurricane Laura makes landfall in Louisiana near the Texas border as a Category 4 storm with 150 mph winds, killing at least 16
AUG 30:	Global cases of COVID-19 pass 25 million with death toll at 843,000
AUG 31:	US cases of COVID-19 pass 6 million with California (699,000) and Florida (619,000) recording the most; number of US COVID-19 deaths reaches 183,300 (Johns Hopkins)

Idea Clustering: Marriage

AUGUST 2, 2020

BETH WEIR

There is a phenomenon I have observed in my suspended Coronavirus life that I am calling idea clustering. By this I mean that disparate notions, seemingly at random but related to a particular idea, come together and demand close examination. Sometimes their appearance is readily explainable. The social and political milieu is an obvious driver, with its focused attention recently on systemic racism. Often the triggers are personal arising from an event, something read or watched.

This is true of my current idea clustering about the institution of marriage. Sadly, the actual triggering event was the sundering apart of lives by death. On Saturday, Bruce and I watched a Zoom celebration of life for Jane, a close friend in Raleigh, NC, whose introvert husband managed, barely, to speak of his love for his wife. His feeling of being bereft could have been bottled and was a singular testament to their relationship.

Since Bruce and I have a wedding anniversary the first week of August and have been chatting about how to celebrate, our sympathy for the grieving spouse was particularly heightened. This one will be our 49th, which is something to celebrate but the lure of the big 50th is somewhat overtaking it. We have managed to do something big on the milestone anniversaries, always travel, beginning with our first—a trip to the UK and US from New Zealand.

On Saturday night we reverted back to Netflix as our default entertainment, tired after the funeral and an afternoon working outside in hot sun. The currently touted *Indian Matchmaking Show* was first to appear on our screen and I was drawn to it immediately. Memories took me there.

When I turned 60, Bruce arranged a trip to India in celebration, a response to my frequently expressed desire to visit. On our first morning in New Delhi, a newspaper was slipped under our hotel door open at the Marriage Section. I took in the columns like lungs take in air and read all of the descriptions of wanted partners. Many of these descriptors, I was to learn, are code for tall, handsome, well-educated, high income, light-skinned and from a good family.

I was particularly intrigued because one of my recent college students, a truly beautiful Indian girl, inside and out, soft spoken and passionate about becoming a teacher, was a partner in an arranged marriage. Her intrigued American classmates had peppered her with questions about it once she gave them permission to do so. She assured them in her regal way that such a pathway to marriage was perfectly proper and she was happy. Certainly she appeared so.

At the first opportunity, when our host in India spoke of his daughter, her husband and grandchildren, I referenced the long columns of advertisements for marriage partners and asked about the custom. Ever mindful of paying respect when in another country, I was relieved when he opened up without hesitation.

"My daughter is a physician," he said as we bounced along the frantic, noisy street in a private car. "I told her that if she finds a partner for a love marriage when at university, that would be fine with me. If not, then I will arrange one when she finishes her training. And that is what happened. She asked me to do so once she qualified. We advertised and liked the family of the first boy who responded. I gave them 20 minutes together." He paused and looked serious. "I would have given them much longer if they had asked."

I later met a woman at a social event with whom I felt 'sympatico' immediately and broached the subject again. I did so this time with more confidence given my earlier reception. She laughed and told me westerners didn't understand the concept of arranged marriages and viewed it as something sinister. She did not see it that way. In her particular case, she and her husband had worked at the same institute and had passed on messages to their respective families that they wanted a formal introduction. Both families were delighted at the outcome. The rest, as the saying goes, is history.

So, who is to know what is the better path? Love or arranged? In any event I got to thinking about my own marriage and what about it I treasure. The early morning cup of tea, certainly; it has shown up as regularly as the dawn. And the last piece of the apple Bruce eats at lunch that he cuts off for me. And that, after being together 24/7 for the last few months, we can still find much to talk about.

My hope is that next year we will be celebrating fifty years, somewhere majestic and interesting and that we can do it without worrying about the damn virus. It has had too much idea clustering already—enough for another one hundred years.

Holler!

AUGUST 11, 2020

WANDA HERNDON

"It's exhausting being Black!"

We share our brilliance, our beauty
touch lives everywhere
but we are absent
from too many places.

We give the world glorious sound
jazz and ragtime
Rhythm & Blues, rap, a touch of Zydeco
and Motown.

No disputing, we provide beats
but imposters make millions
We suffer under their feet
Casualties of their greed.

We holler, "It's exhausting being Black!"

We clench our teeth
suppress our rage
expose the vultures
who steal our culture.

Repeat our stories
Raise our voices, increase the chatter
Continue saying why Black Lives Matter
Try not to explode.

We do our best
Sick of waging battles
that do not bring change.
We wish to rest.

Believe when we say,
"It's exhausting being Black!"

Birthday Party: Short, Outside, Distanced

AUGUST 27, 2020

LAURA CELISE LIPPMAN

Stay Home Stay Safe
alarm call of the 3-year-old
birthday boy to his slightly
older encroaching cousins.

A megaphone voice of fear
from a tiny guy echoing
the mantra of his days.
The 5-year-old replies

matter-of-factly
with his standard line;
the coronavirus you mean
followed by the 4-year-old;

yeah COVID-19. Back to play—
further apart as long as it sustains
maybe five short minutes
'til the line gets breached again.

The party was short—outside, distanced,
ventilated by a soft ocean breeze.
Now, days later, I sit under the shadow
of the Liars Convention where the cloud

that hangs over us is glibly
ignored in favor of the soaring
stocks of the one percent.
The silence, with the boys gone,

is profound, lonely and hollow.
The lapping waves remind me
that water finds its level
and lets me hope
for a new tomorrow.

SEPTEMBER 2020

SEP 1: President Trump visits the city of Kenosha, Wisconsin, where Jacob Blake was shot, to offer support for law enforcement

SEP 3: Copernicus Atmosphere Monitoring Service reports the Arctic Circle has worst fire season on record

SEP 3: MacKenzie Scott, philanthropist and ex-wife of Amazon CEO Jeff Bezos, becomes the world's richest woman, worth $68 billion

SEP 4: Record 52% of US 18–29-year-olds are living with their parents because of the pandemic (Pew Research Center Study)

SEP 5: More than 50 arrested as Portland, Oregon, marks 100 days of protests against racism and police brutality

SEP 6: Strain of bacteria nicknamed Conan the Bacterium survives three years attached to the International Space Station in open space

SEP 6: Los Angeles County reported its highest-ever temperature of 121° F

SEP 7: India overtakes Brazil to record the second-highest number of COVID-19 cases with 4.2 million

SEP 7: Wildfires have burned a record 2 million acres in California 2020 fire season

SEP 8: Moria refugee camp, Europe's biggest migrant camp, burns down on the Greek island of Lesbos, leaving 13,000 people without shelter

SEP 9: Global death toll from COVID-19 passes 900,000; US has the most deaths at 190,589

SEP 10: Wildfires in Oregon cause 500,000 people to evacuate—more than 10% of the state's population—with an unprecedented 900,000 acres burned

SEP 10: California's August Complex wildfire becomes largest recorded in state history at 736 square miles

SEP 14: WHO reports largest-ever one-day COVID-19 case rise of

307,930; daily death toll of 5,500 and overall death total of 917,417

SEP 15: *Scientific American* issues its first ever presidential endorsement in 175 years by backing Joe Biden

SEP 19: President Trump vows to swear in a new Supreme Court judge, despite the election being only 45 days away

SEP 22: US COVID-19 death toll passes 200,000, more than any other country

SEP 23: Kentucky grand jury indicts one of three officers for wanton engagement for shooting unarmed Breonna Taylor in Louisville

SEP 23: President Trump refuses to commit to a peaceful transfer of power after the US November election at a White House conference

SEP 24: President Trump nominates Judge Amy Coney Barrett for the US Supreme Court to replace Ruth Bader Ginsburg

SEP 25: Justice Ruth Bader Ginsburg becomes the first woman to lie in state in the US Capitol in Washington D.C.

SEP 28: COVID-19 recorded global death toll passes one million with over 33 million known cases

SEP 30: California becomes the first US state to pass a law allowing reparations for Black residents and descendants of slaves

Why Make a Plan?

SEPTEMBER 11, 2020

JANE SPALDING

Shambolic. Of British origin meaning obviously disorganized or confused.

President Obama used the word to describe "Trump's shambolic approach to government." Today, nineteen years after the shambolic collapse of the Twin Towers in New York City, people who lost homes in wildfires in Washington, Oregon and California have an intimate knowledge of the word shambles and all its iterations and synonyms.

The shambolicness of my life pales in comparison. In another time I would have used the word tongue in cheek to describe my recent attempts to make plans in spite of the shambles. Today it's a stretch to find the humor.

"How do you make plans when it's impossible to make plans?" asks Cindy Lamonthe in a *New York Times* article, "How to Cope when Everything Keeps Changing," September 7, 2020.

"The ground beneath our feet is constantly shifting. Planning for anything more than a week out can feel futile—almost silly—since no one knows what the next week, much less the next month, will bring. A surge in coronavirus cases in your area? More lockdowns? Worrying about natural disasters?"

Today I planned to work in my garden with Tim. A super-massive smoke plume blew into Seattle, along with dire warnings about being outside, upending that plan. Thanks to wildfires raging in the West, the sky looks like an overcast, fogged-in January day. Only fog doesn't bring with it an otherworldly orangeish glow. Or smell like fire, or cause the eyes to burn, or the throat to feel scratchy.

In the past two weeks one plan did go exceptionally well. Nick orchestrated the move out of his Whidbey Island home of the past 15 years pretty brilliantly. He divided the contents of his 4,000 square foot house into at least 5 piles—one to give away, books to donate to the library sale, things to take to my house for a two-month stay, other things for a five-month stay at a beach house in Langley, and things to leave for his daughter and her family who are moving into his home. He spent a lot of time organizing, sorting, planning, giving away, moving stuff from a giveaway pile to a keep pile and back again, until the day arrived the movers came and installed the first wave of furniture and boxes in a storage unit. The plan? To move into my home in Seattle for two months, then to a Whidbey Island home on the beach for five months.

So, we made a plan. It didn't get off to a great start. Workers were in my home replacing the large living room window, a project delayed by five months because of the early March shutdown on construction. We arrived at a house whose front was covered in scaffolding, and whose insides were discombobulated and covered in dust. The room that was to become Nick's was filled with everything that didn't fit anywhere else.

In the meantime, Lexi, the college student who lived in my home over the summer, planned to move into a house with three other students on Sept. 1. Shortly before Nick moved out of his house, she told me two of the students weren't coming back from their home in Hawaii because the university had just announced that all their classes would be online. A week later, after finding the perfect two-bedroom apartment, she learned that Dad of the fourth roommate wouldn't pay for her rent. After a serious discussion about how we would manage COVID precautions, I agreed she could stay in my house.

So far, we've survived a shambolic move along with Nick's feelings of grief for his island home, his acute awareness of the noise of the city, and not having a place to put his stuff. The workers are gone now, the house is back together, and Nick has a room of his own. We're creating new routines and patterns in our days. Lexi is a considerate roommate.

And then there's my daughter who decided to come home after one more breakup with the boyfriend. So now I find myself in the unwarranted position of being the COVID exposure manager of the pod I so carefully created.

Prepare for the new normal they say. How do you prepare for a life that warns against making plans? That puts me in a position of deciding whether my daughter can live in my home? That piles natural disaster on a pandemic with a ridiculous lack of leadership from our president?

An article by Tara Haelle in an article called "Your 'Surge Capacity' Is Depleted—It's Why You Feel Awful" published in *Medium*, August 16, 2020, offers some help. She says, "I might have intellectually accepted back in March that the next two years (or more?) are going to be nothing like normal, and not even predictable in how they won't be normal. But cognitively recognizing and accepting that fact and emotionally incorporating that reality into everyday life aren't the same. Our new normal is always feeling a little off balance, like trying to stand in a dinghy on rough seas, and not knowing when the storm will pass. But humans can get better at anything with practice."

She offers some well-researched practical suggestions, but that is food for another musing.

Psilocybe Love Story

SEPTEMBER 12, 2020

LAURA CELISE LIPPMAN

I dread winter this year.
After our summer of virus,
the joys of outdoor gatherings
are smothered by smoke.

Now more than ever
the encroaching dark & thoughts
of boots squelching over mud
threaten my composure.

Rain-filled rivers will flow high
Long after summer flames are doused.
Lush underbrush will spring back
from summer crush in greening woods.

Short days loom wet & gray, though psilocybes
wait to be plucked under cow-dung pancakes.
Raindrops may be sipped like ambrosia
from moss sponges & lichen cups.

My dread of the wet season
morphs into lovely mushroom memories;
I dream back to the first autumn that
my loving partner joined me in the West.

We reunited in the moist luxuriance
of the deep Olympic rainforest
near the vast Pacific Ocean;
magical futures unfurled before us.

Botanical resonance with communal
memories sprung from deep wells
of tribal archetypes & visions
spilled over iron red cliffs.

Rivers of energy flowed
like blood over spirits

of grand and ancient cedars
washed in from the sea.

Intrepid totems of hope and strength,
I look to them for sustenance during difficult days ahead.

Words, Words, Words

SEPTEMBER 22, 2020

TYSON GREER

Lexicographers must be having a field day. The OED has been busy adding and redefining terms but threw up its collective hands at the prospect of naming its traditional "word of the year" for 2020.

This year, with the spotlight on pestilence and racism—the latter a new horse for the Apocalypse—our language stretched to define this notnormal time. Language is a living thing—it evolves to meet new challenges.

Coronaviruses, as every five-year-old now knows, are a large family of viruses that cause a wide spectrum of symptoms... none of them desirable, some downright deadly. The full name, if you have lexicography-leanings is severe acute respiratory syndrome coronavirus 2 (a.k.a. SARS-CoV-2), which doesn't really roll off the tongue.

The World Health Organization christened the virus that first appeared in China's Hubei Province in 2019 as "COVID-19" not only because it was catchy, but primarily because it was easy to pronounce and because it does not imply (or blame) any people, places, or animals. Of course, someone living in the White House zoomed right past this and into dark waters.

The word "Zoom" is no longer a toddler's imitation of a Hot Wheels car racing around the living room. Zoom begat "Zoom-bombing." In the early days (February, March) of the explosion of Zoom meetings, the software "permitted" uninvited guests to disrupt zoom meetings with offensive behavior or language. (That bug has been fixed.) Zoombombing is a variant of "photobombing."

"Zooming" includes all kinds of virtual meetings, e.g. for those WFH (working-from-home...or at least trying to while juggling their toddlers with Hot Wheels, kids' Zoom-school, and Zoom-playdates). The term "Zoom mom" is an update of the suburban term "soccer mom." Zoom moms are a potentially powerful voting bloc in the 2020 elections.

Zoom-time also spawned the term "Virtual Happy Hour," as an obvious necessity (particularly for WFHs) once the bars (and bars pretending to be restaurants) were closed. On a healthier note, our Yoga class quickly squeezed its tights into a Zoom-room, and Zoom-Yoga became my favorite oxymoron. (It works, except for hearing Ahhhh-Ohhhhh-Mmmmmmmmm on those tinny computer speakers.)

By April, signs began appearing on bus sides and highway readerboards urging people to "Stay Home. Stay Safe." The term "Shelter-in-Place" was pressed into service from its role in hurricanes and other natural disasters. I found "S-i-P" to be cozier than its cousin "Self-isolate," which I find clinical and just plain awkward. Both of these terms imply a voluntary, self-preserving confinement.

The word "Quarantine" is a chill wind. Nothing friendly about it. You are "locked down" and going to stay that way for 14 days, or face consequences. Of course, during quarantine, you might enjoy a "Quarantini"—shaken or stirred? And that beverage may be taken, once you are released, as a "walktail," a term for taking a walk (getting exercise, that's admirable) with a drink in your hand that isn't from Starbucks.

Speaking of exercise, another popular term is "COVID-10" or "COVID-15" or, worse, "COVID-20," referring to the 10, 15, or 20 pounds gained by staying home, with not enough distance from the refrigerator. The phrase "flatten the curve" is not affiliated with Weight Watchers.

"Quaranteam" is a blend of quarantine and team, which refers to that special, and by definition small, group of friends and/or family members with whom you feel safe, because you trust they abide by the same safety "rules" as you do. Its synonym "pod" harkens back to "peas in a ...". And "bubble"... still makes me think of champagne.

Trust has also become an important word, important to our continued safety. Not everyone lives by the same "rules." I still bristle when I encounter a "covidiot," a person who disregards public health advice (or mandates), such as wearing a PPE (Personal Protective Equipment you wear on your face, not...) and maintaining "social distancing." That latter term has been turned upside down since its first use in the 1950s, when "socially distant" described an aloof person.

While I haven't seen anyone try to shake hands since February, I'm not comfortable with the "elbow bump," which some people seem to feel is a safe alternative. Actually, it's not, and hasn't been since the rule for "cover your cough" no longer meant cover your cough with your hand, and polite people adhere to coughing into their elbow. And this elbow is what you want to bump? "Foot bumps" came briefly into fashion in China but made little headway here.

Unfortunately, when the CDC worked up their communications protocol to provide uniform messaging to the public—a primary responsibility of the CDC—about the threat and precautions, they jumped on "six feet" of "Social Distancing." I don't know if others felt uncomfortable with the "six feet" reference—it reminded me immediately of "six feet under," not a good place to be. (Unfortunate that CDC never married those two thoughts—it might have added weight to their messaging. I do think "mask it or casket" is catchy.)

Back in March, experts around the world reported that six feet was not enough—10 or 12 feet was more realistic protection. In the last week, CDC has changed its mind more than a teenage girl changes her outfits.

But words are not like a car, which can be recalled. Conflicting words cause confusion and add to the stress. As if the wildfires and smoke and racial equality and the election—and this week, the death of RBG—weren't enough bad news stress-triggers.

When I was a child, my babysitter, a sweet, white-haired soul, read the back page of the *Baltimore Sun*, which chronicled the murders, stabbings, fires, and she kept muttering "Ain't it awful. Ain't it awful." Our equivalent today is "Doom-scrolling." Scrolling through the legions of awful news. Sometimes not even reading the articles, just scrolling from terrible headline to horrible headline.

It's under these pressures that many people have outbreaks of "caution exhaustion." Tired of masks, tired of take-out, tired of precautions, tired of bad news.

Today is Fall Equinox, the time to remember the renewal of fall. As we transition indoors, we'll remember to read and seek out and strive to be the writers who take the long view, and see beyond the horizon of chaos, constraints, lies, and despair. And, like Shakespeare, make up words and stories to get us through the long winter ahead, until we can fully embrace Spring.

Would Our Divide Narrow if We Just Talked—and Listened

SEPTEMBER 26, 2020

BETH WEIR

Note from the author: My writing buddies persuaded me to send this essay to the local paper, The Seattle Times, *when I brought it to the group. It was published in the Opinion Section, September 26, 2020, under the auspice of 'My Take,' set aside for personal essays. I was delighted when it was printed, as that was unexpected.*

The first time my spouse and I came to America, the country was roiling with the scandal that became known as Watergate. The fierce, animated kitchen table discussions we were party to served as my introduction to the politics of the country.

Later, not long after Watergate was settled, we emigrated from New Zealand to live in the US. By chance, we bought into a street with immigrants from China, Japan, Germany and India along with two Black and five white families. Our collective children played in the cul-de-sac together and put on dreadful plays. Then, and on many cooling summer evenings, the neighbors gathered casually and talked about the trivial to the consequential. In short, I experienced the concept of the melting pot in the real world. I heard all the stories.

My personal experience as a naturalized American has been immensely fulfilling but I've become uncomfortable over the time I have lived in the US about the growing number, native born and otherwise, who are not finding a place in society. The Social Progress Index, a survey of 163 countries, released September 10, 2020 has verified why that feeling has grown. The issues examined are those that contribute to the quality of life: nutrition, safety, freedom, health, education access, etc. The US ranks overall at 28th out of 163 countries and has seen, along with Brazil and Hungary, the biggest decline in our quality of life since 2011. Then we were 19th in the world. If you want to live in a country with a high social-progress score, you have a choice of Norway, Denmark, Finland or New Zealand.

To be sure our universities are No.1, but access to a solid public education is ranked at 91—at a par with Uzbekistan and Mongolia. Most other advanced countries have better sanitation and Internet access and have laws against child marriage. (Many states still allow it in some circumstances in the US.) America ranks 100 in discrimination against minorities. Health statistics in the US are similar to those of Chile, Jordan and Albania.

Obviously, this state of affairs has happened over time and under both red and blue administrations. But the current political divide has never been this great or so mindlessly vitriolic in the fifty years I have observed it. I cannot but think this breakdown is driven, in part, by the fact that too many live in third world conditions. Simply, hungry and insecure people are going to be angry. A quick test of this hypothesis: try asking anyone in need of help through no fault of their own and not getting it, how they feel. Or talk to someone who has lost health insurance as a result of the pandemic or will if Obamacare is struck down in court as unconstitutional.

Where do we start to address these social progress issues? There are solutions given political will and a more receptive disposition to the 'common good' than currently exists. But as neither seem within reach just now, I would like to suggest a version of the 'talking on the street to people who don't look like you' approach. A hallmark of my early neighborhood conversations that were frequently feisty, was a slow, respectful unfolding of the various points of view offered. It offered considerable understanding. I have no idea how this could be implemented in the US but a formal version of the approach known as the Truth and Reconciliation Commission went a long way in South Africa to bind the apartheid wounds. But something like it is what I hope for the country I have adopted and grown to love. To do less is to risk much.

More Cases of COVID

SEPTEMBER 30, 2020

MARY ANN GONZALES

United States Daily Cases of COVID-19 on Sept 1—31,535

September has always been a great month for me. My birthday is September 1. School started days later, and New Yellow pencils were high on my "happy list." We did not get new clothes because in all Catholic schools, we wore uniforms.

This COVID September was continuing to grow cases of infection, but I took a leap of faith and went to my hair stylist and got my hair cut. Doesn't seem like a big deal, but when I took a step back and realized that I had no human touch since March, it seemed I wanted and needed to have some contact. I looked like an ancient crone with not enough ego to take care of myself.

"AAAAH," I said and leaned into the experience.

We have begun to get smoke from the horrific fires burning on the West Coast. The sky is orangey and other worldly. We just finished painting my daughter's house and found the air less pristine than our usual breezy Puget Sound freshness. It was hard not to worry excessively about those poor folks losing everything in the conflagrations.

On the day I got my flu shot (9-22-20) the US passed 7.2 million cases of COVID-19: deaths now up to 22,300 souls. How we wish for a vaccine. Trump keeps promising one is available "just around the corner," but the facts do not support his words. Even if the scientists develop one, the timeline for wide distribution is quite a way down the lane.

But, as the cases and deaths pile up in horrifying numbers month by month, life goes on. Birthdays, doctor appointments, football, house repairs, coffee outdoors with friends. But all life has changed. The isolation, fear, depression begin to take their toll as the weather turns colder and outside "meets" get more difficult.

I am beginning to accept, even appreciate the ZOOM experience. I was a troglodyte, a non-complaint hold-out, but now when options are scarce, I grudgingly accept it because it gets me at least the sight and sound of others in my world.

In the process of developing a "Trust" for my assets, I find myself spelunking through the files for my will, the Neptune Society contract, the DNR (Do Not Resuscitate) documents. I discover the documents I prepared for my kids, including the card I thought they might use as a "Celebration of my Death" party and a last note of love to them. I plan to outlive this pandemic, but the proximity to these files does lead me to take note of my possible outcomes.

(As I am typing, I hear a sound of a train barreling down the street. Well, no, it is not a train it is a real doozy of a rainstorm starting at the South end of my block and just now hitting my house. I take it to be a reminder of the ferocity of this virus and how it spreads with such velocity.)

There are joys, however. The color of leaves as they change to a glorious crimson and dance in the wind; the day I beat out the rain and got the final coat of paint on the window trim; the call from my granddaughter to ask if they got tested could they come visit. Some of which I might have overlooked before COVID-19.

United States Daily Cases of COVID-19 on Sept 30—43,114

OCTOBER 2020

OCT 1:   White House aide Hope Hicks tests positive for COVID-19

OCT 2:   President Trump tweets that he and First Lady Melania tested positive for COVID-19. Then he is admitted to Walter Reed Military Medical Center

OCT 3:   At least 10 people in President Trump's inner circle have tested positive for the virus

OCT 5:   At least 14 tons of microplastics reside in ocean sediment, 30 times more than on the surface, according to new research on the Great Australian Bight

OCT 5:   WHO estimates 10% of the planet's population may have been infected with COVID-19, more than 20 times number of confirmed cases.

OCT 5:   Death toll in India passes 100,000, 3rd highest in the world; Brazil is #2; US is still #1

OCT 5:   President Trump left Walter Reed while still infectious and returned to White House; 200,000 have died in US

OCT 6:   President Trump announced he is suspending COVID-19 relief talks until after the election

OCT 7:   Hurricane Delta hits Mexico's Yucatan Peninsula, 25th named storm for this year

OCT 8:   FBI charges 13 men with plotting to kidnap Michigan Governor Gretchen Whitmer and storm the Michigan Capital

OCT 9:   Nobel Peace Prize awarded to The UN's World Food Program

OCT 12:   After a dozen cases were discovered in the City of Quindao, Chinese government will test the entire population (9 million) within 5 days

OCT 14:   As cases surge, French president Emmanuel Macron declares a public health emergency and a 9 pm curfew for nine cities

OCT 14:   A copy of William Shakespeare's First Folio sells for a record $9.98 million at NY auction

OCT 14:	YouTube announced ban of false COVID vaccination videos, in effort to eliminate misinformation
OCT 17:	New Zealand's Prime Minister Jacinda Ardern re-elected in a landslide
OCT 20:	Argentine becomes 5th country in the world to record over 1 million confirmed COVID-19 cases
OCT 20:	US Justice Department sues Google for illegal monopoly over search and search advertising
OCT 21:	The parents of 545 children separated from their parents at the US-Mexico border cannot be found (ACLU)
OCT 21:	FBI reports Iran and Russia hacked US voter information to influence 2020 election
OCT 22:	Goldman Sachs agrees to pay $3 billion in 1Malaysia Development Berhad (1MBD) corruption scandal
OCT 23:	Dr. Anthony Fauci suggested it was time for a US mask mandate due to rising cases: 83,010 cases reported in 24 hours (441,541 cases in US)
OCT 26:	Philadelphia police shoot and kill Walter Wallace Jr, a Black man armed with a knife, prompting protests and city-wide curfew
OCT 26:	Melbourne ends three-month lockdown after no new cases of COVID-19 since June
OCT 26:	Japanese PM Yoshihide Suga reports the country will be carbon neutral by 2050
OCT 27:	US Senate confirms Amy Coney Barrett to Supreme Court, ensuring a conservative majority
OCT 27:	A week before election day, a record 69.5 million Americans have voted
OCT 27:	WHO confirms Europe experiencing 2nd COVID-19 wave, 30% new cases a week, deaths rising 40%
OCT 28:	Worldwide COVID-19 cases rose 25% in less than 2 weeks, one-day increase tops 500,000 for first time

OCT 29: India reports over 8 million COVID-19 cases, 2nd to US, with death toll of 120,527

OCT 30: UK PM Boris Johnson issues a second 4-week lockdown for England

Calculated Risk is the New Now

OCTOBER 4, 2020

JANE SPALDING

On the chaotic day in late August when Nick moved out of his Whidbey Island home and into mine, which was in total disarray from the Great 2020 Window Replacement Project underway there, I called Kalaloch Lodge. We needed a break. I remembered staying in cozy cabins on this wild beach on the Pacific Ocean in Olympic National Park years ago. Thinking it would be a COVID-safe getaway: a day's drive from Seattle, privacy in the cabins, and lots of fresh air, I made reservations for the earliest date available, a month away.

I carefully requested a cabin on the bluff with a full kitchen and made peace with the exorbitant price of $350/night. As the time approached, I happened upon a Trip Advisor review of our reserved accommodations. How disappointing to find one review after another stating that the cabins were not clean. Not clean? In this time of virus paranoia? Not only that, the kitchen was not well supplied said one reviewer, and the knives were not sharp said another. The final indignity: on check-in you received a package of compostable dishes and utensils, the kind where the spoon melts into a bowl of hot soup and you drink coffee from plasticized Styrofoam.

Nick, who has no allegiance to Kalaloch, said the obvious, "Why would we go there?"

"Because it's the only place you can stay in the park that's on a wild beach," I wailed.

"Let's just check it out," he said with his resolute calmness.

A search through Airbnb turned up a variety of cute touristy places under $300/night. We settled on one on a lake near Port Angeles and booked it. Then I read the fine print. Three times. Each time it said there is no running water. Incredulous I called Judy, the owner.

"Yes," she said matter of factly, "there is no running water. We provide 30 gallons to wash the dishes and there is a waterless composting toilet with peat moss that works pretty well."

"Uh...so there's no way to take a shower?" I asked.

"Well most people stay two or three nights and I guess they're OK not taking a shower. Or there's an outdoor portable water bag. And you can just rinse off in the lake. Oh yes, there is a steep walk downhill to get to the lake," she added cheerily.

"I don't think this is going to work for us," I said calmly, when what I really wanted to say was, "You don't think you could have put this upfront in the property description!"

"Oh, just contact Airbnb," she said "they'll give you a refund. Call me if you have any problems."

"You have to ask if the place you want to stay has running water?" I fumed as I began dialing. I was determined to get a person on the phone at Airbnb. Now I'm persistent with big corporations and the obnoxious grilling their robots do to prevent you from getting to a person. I waited six hours for a return call from Delta Airlines to get a flight out of COVID-infested Italy in March. I spent half a day on hold to get a person from Apple on the phone when I spilled coffee on my computer. I must say, Airbnb wins the prize for the most offensive customer service. Ever. I chose every option they gave me and there was no way to talk to a person! The system sent me over and over again through text messages and emails to their refund page. There they offered half of the $500+ I had just spent on the reservation.

I took a deep breath and called Judy. "Oh," she said, "I thought they had a grace period for cancellations." I asked her if she would refund the amount that Airbnb wouldn't. "Yes," she said. I decided to trust that half the refund would come from Judy, half from Airbnb. It did.

Restored to rational thinking I said to Nick, "Let's try Forks. We'll just drive to the wild and wonderful beaches." We turned up several cute touristy fishing cabins, then found a whole house listed for $91. What caught my attention, other than the price, was not how it looked, but that every review mentioned how clean the place was. When we read about the recently remodeled kitchen and bathroom, we booked it.

Sunday, we drove to Forks making numerous stops along the way. First, to my favorite Costco in Sequim, a popular retirement community on the Olympic Peninsula. Costco wouldn't ordinarily make the list of tourist attractions, but these are no ordinary times. The Sequim Costco is super friendly and not crowded. Craving a hotdog and pizza, and several favorite items we had done without since the stay-at-home order in March, we were practically giddy...going to Costco for heaven's sake. Everyone inside wore masks. No one offered food samples, nor was there any place to sit down and enjoy Costco's culinary treats.

The exit checker offered a sign of life before COVID-19. To people leaving the big box store she said, "I know where you'll be at 1:30." I asked what's happening at 1:30 and she said, "The Seahawks are playing." Duh! I hadn't noticed customers in their blue and green Seahawks garb. Watching the Seahawks play football is what people used to do on Sunday afternoons in September.

Next stop, on this glorious afternoon, Dungeness Spit with its wild waves, sunshine, and high tide. Then, on to Forks, home to 3,600 people. Once the logging capital of the world, the town surged in popularity fifteen years ago when the Twilight series of books about a young girl and her attraction to vampires became a teenage craze. Now entry to the visitor's center is blocked by a young lady standing in front of a card table. No one is permitted to go inside to take selfies with life size cardboard cutouts of Bella, Edward and Jacob, heroes from the Twilight books. Signs supporting Trump and Culp pepper the area. Not one supported Joe Biden or Jay Inslee.

A six-foot cactus handcrafted out of crinkly fabric and hundreds of beads and baubles greeted us from the garden across the street from our Airbnb. As reported, our home, one of about fifty in the Forks Mobile Home Park, was shiny clean and perfectly comfortable. The refrigerator still had manufacturer's stickers on it. The inside of the home was a blur of brown, carefully fabricated to look like real wood walls and floors and real leather furniture. A wood plaque, along with a pair of antlers on the wall, reminded us we were in hunting country. The plaque listed symptoms of:

Buck Fever:
- Rapid Pulse
- The Shakes
- Weak at the Knees
- Double Vision
- Brain Dead.

There Ain't No Cure

Not to be confused with COVID Fever!

Forks turned out to be the perfect starting place to visit Ruby Beach. After hiking downhill and maneuvering across driftwood logs, we luxuriated on the stone-filled beach in view of a rock formation called Abbey Island. Last stop of the day was a secluded part of Kalaloch Beach where, so in love with the moment, we both stripped down to nothing and ran into the freezing waters of the Pacific Ocean.

Refreshed and replenished by the beautiful beaches, topped off by a visit to the top of Hurricane Ridge on a clear day, we reluctantly made our way back to Seattle. Distracted from the reaction to the sad death of our beloved Ruth Bader Ginsburg, and horrified by the first presidential debate, we braced for the next national disaster—the president had COVID-19. Our outing away from the safety of our homes was a perfect reminder that nature offers constancy, in spite of the backdrop of human folly.

Midnight

OCTOBER 6, 2020

WANDA HERNDON

Hours past midnight uninvited guests arrive,
inject deadly venom into my dreams
I am vulnerable, nothing is as it seems.

Poisonous snakes puncture my skin
trap me in a nightmare with horrible fiends
I can't see them, feel them, I scream, I scream.

Chaos snuffs out coherent thoughts
my body shakes, constricted, without cover
while demons levitate, menacingly hover.

Restless hours, bathed in sweat, chase slumber
until whispered courage shakes me awake.
Translucent pythons slowly ascend, dissipate.

Sleep falls from my tired red eyes
Thank you, dear savior, unholy snakes are gone.
My eyes wide open to a glorious new dawn.

Love provides comfort, wrapped in its glow
foes defeated, now only peaceful dreams.
I have limitless power; I am stronger than I seem.

Making 2020 Add Up

OCTOBER 6, 2020

BETH WEIR

Legend says it's impossible to count the stones that comprise the ancient monument of Stonehenge, since every attempt to do so yields a different result. The year of 2020 feels a bit like that. It is enormously difficult to make it add up, no matter how hard you try. The adjective that rises above all else is exhausting.

Until October. While out walking Jack, Bruce had a discussion with two neighbors about Scotch. It turns out they like it and so do we. So we invited Joie and Charles for a tasting on our patio.

In the course of the visit, I asked Joie, a dean in the UW School of Nursing, some questions about the history of nursing education. This conversational turn came about because I had been researching the subject as part of my sanity-saving project in 2020: writing a novel. One of the characters, Annette, is an ambitious young woman who trained as a nurse in the late 1940s and early 1950s.

Joie suggested I contact three of her former colleagues for background information. Two are in their 80s and one is 98. Individually their experiences in training differed. One began in the nurse cadet program; the others earned university degrees. The 'nurse cadet' ultimately earned her master's, the other two doctorates.

I was amused when I set up the visits or phone calls since each woman responded to my email inquiry the same way. Let me check my calendar to see when I am available. Can only hope I'll be as spry when the time comes, I thought.

In my conversations with the women, I encountered great joy despite their increasing frailties. They are still united in their passion for nursing, their groundbreaking experiences and their scoffing of longago conventions. I quote Marge who said, "if I was waiting by the elevator and a doctor happened along, he got to use it and I had to wait until it returned." Her chuckles following that comment were more scornful than any remark would have been.

Doris, the eldest, started out as a nurse cadet and married a soldier halfway through her training so had to leave because of her changed status. When her husband died in combat, she finished the program and kept on 'finishing.'

Pam had a plea that I didn't expect but made sense given her personal experiences. She asked me to make the character in the novel an intelligent nurse. She wanted to see Annette as a woman with careful respect for the job she is doing and who was not letting herself be defined by the expectations of others.

It was a wonderful feeling being in the orbit of such solid women. They cannot make 2020 add up but they sure helped.

Fortunately, the month has another treat in store. Our immediate neighbor has a warehouse attic of frightful monsters, dripping blood and eyeballs that he puts out every October for Halloween. It is so vivid and arresting a display it is regularly featured on television. Certainly it brings on massive viewing crowds. Setting it up takes a month of Saturdays and Sundays. This weekend Doug started work and that very act made me smile. It also helped me make 2020 add up.

Awe Walks

OCTOBER 12, 2020

LAURA CELISE LIPPMAN

We took the kids
when we could
outside to the woods.

Little moments of awe
made what we saw
a balance to our daily dread.

There was iridescent mud
underfoot in a special place
near the permanent puddle
under the weeds invading the space.

The swooping owl's looming grace
as it startled from its tree
scared complacency out of me.

We especially loved slimy slugs,
more substantial than airy bugs
and sea stars returning
from their viral churning.

The moon snail's band of mantle
burrowed beneath grains of sands.
The seal and her babe
bobbed on waves

and made our day feel sweet.
In that special way orcas cavort
they help us forget the steely fortress
of our newly shrunken world.

My doctor prescribes
the Awe Walk
when my mood balks and dives.

A meditative nature prayer,
better than pills and wine,
a nature song among whispering
trees' towering altars
sighs between breathing beats
of heaving weaving waves.

Caution Exhaustion

OCTOBER 20, 2020

TYSON GREER

At the end of October, it's not goblins, ghosts, and ghouls we might open our door to—it's COVID. I don't mean the kids are trading it for treats—I mean we need to be cautious, very cautious. (And if that phrase echoes in your mind as "Be afraid, very afraid," I'm with you.)

The thing is, the summer of 2020, while not exactly the "summer of love," is going to seem like that compared to Fall, when the sun sleeps in later and later, and cringes lower and lower in the Northwest sky, and tucks below the horizon earlier and earlier. And the rains begin. And it's damp and cold outside.

In July, I looked ahead. I had visions that when September would roll into October, and October bow out to November, we'd still have a very few people over in the back yard, safely-distanced (S-D). I told anyone who would listen, "Hey, we'll just put on coats, and mittens, and scarves, and hats and enjoy getting together on the patio under the covered deck. No problem. Might have to get some kind of heater, but heck—we're resilient. We can do this!"

A week ago, a friend came over and we sat S-D on separate benches outside chatting and enjoying the garden. The Burning Bush lived up to its name, its fire-red leaves contrasted brightly with the flame-yellow Osier Dogwood, and the final burst of burgundy-orange dahlias nodded their heads companionably. But as the afternoon went on, I noticed the colors drained into the grayscale of twilight. With jackets and shawls we were physically warm enough...maybe it would be better in the middle of the day.

Today, an overcast day expected to be in the low 50s (there have been July days in the mid-50s), our writing group decided that sitting outside bundled up for a two-hour meeting didn't sound like fun. To my surprise, I agreed. October days without bright sun are bone-chilling. And what we want is warmth.

By November, we will be desperately seeking the warmth of live contact with friends and family. But my good-sense-self tells me we have to continue to be cautious about what constitutes risk, and, on a day-to-day basis, decide how much risk we're willing to afford. The COVID numbers are rising.

Enter "caution-exhaustion." Truth is: We're tired of being cautious. Tired of that edgy feeling as you navigate the aisles of a grocery store on the alert to the closeness of strangers. Many of us have become "hypervigilant," a word I didn't know before October. People report generalized anxiety and problems with sleep, tossing and turning, wrapped tight in existential dread. Sleep used to "knit up the ravell'ed sleeve of care," but COVID murders sleep.

As the opportunities to be with family and friends diminish in Fall and Winter, I think about how we connect. It was easy in the "before time." You meet for coffee. You cheer at the kids' games. Loudly. You go out to dinner or come over for supper. You linger at the Thanksgiving table or the Boxing Day brunch. You sing carols. Loudly. Not this year.

But it's only one year... probably. I can do one year. The bargain is: one year of caution for many more years of ... everything. In the meantime, I can gladly bundle up and sit outside to be with our growing-tall grandsons. I can crank up the optimism machine and inhale its sweetness. I can do this.

Even More Cases of COVID-19

OCTOBER 31, 2020

MARY ANN GONZALES

United States Daily Cases of COVID-19 on October 1, 2020: 43,981

President Trump announced that he and Melania have COVID. My emotions were varied: I did not wish him dead, but I did want him to suffer a bit. Suffer as those who he just blew off as he told us repeatedly, "We are turning the corner."

He was given all the possible drugs available only to him and he declared himself "Fine." We never heard him mention the First Lady or his aide Hope Hicks, or Kellyanne Conway or Chris Christie as they also were infected.

He does keep promising a vaccine, "Just around the corner," he says. He calls it Operation Warp Speed. But so far, the facts do not support his words.

I feel like the proverbial deer in the headlights unable to make a move. There are chores to accomplish that seem too enormous to even contemplate starting. I delay. I "bury my head in the sand," then I give myself Stern Talkings To. Subsequently I feel bad about my inability to overcome the "Laziness!"

How typical.

P.S. If you read Louise Penny's books, you know that FINE means: Fucked Up, Insecure, Neurotic and Egotistical.

United States Daily Cases of COVID 19 on October 31, 2020: 90,807

NOVEMBER 2020

NOV 1:   Early voting in US continues

NOV 3:   US presidential and down-ballot elections held throughout country

NOV 7:   Former Vice President Joe Biden declared the apparent winner of the US presidential race, defeating sitting President Donald Trump

NOV 8:   Global recorded cases of COVID-19 pass 50 million, with the known death toll at 1,245,240 (Johns Hopkins data)

NOV 8:   Rudy Giuliani holds infamous Trump Campaign press conference at the Four Seasons Total Landscaping in Philadelphia to contest US election results

NOV 9:   US records more than 10 million COVID-19 cases with one million new cases recorded in 10 days. Death toll is over 237,000

NOV 9:   Drug makers BioNTech and Pfizer announce their COVID-19 vaccine to be over 90% effective in a first look at the results from their phase 3 trials involving nearly 44,000 people

NOV 9:   US Attorney General William Barr controversially approves federal investigations into voter fraud for the US elections

NOV 10:   Word of the year is "lockdown" according to Collins English Dictionary

NOV 12:   Senator Kamala Harris makes US history as the first woman and first woman of color to be elected to the vice presidency

NOV 14:   Record global daily total of 660,905 COVID-19 cases declared (WHO)

NOV 15:   President Trump tweets Biden won because the election was rigged, while still refusing to concede the election

NOV 18:   US COVID-19 death toll passes 250,000, recorded cases at 11.5 million, and hospitalizations at 76,830 amid a country-wide surge

NOV 23: US President-elect Joe Biden introduces his new cabinet including Alejandro Mayorkas, first Latino head of homeland security, and Avril Haines, first female director of national intelligence

NOV 24: US General Services Administration officially begins Joe Biden's transition, declaring him the apparent winner although Donald Trump vows to continue challenging the result

NOV 24: COVID-19 surge in the US with one-day death toll of 2,200 highest since May and new cases averaging 175,000 a day

NOV 29: Joe Biden and Kamala Harris announce the first all-female communications team

NOV 30: Joe Biden announces he is nominating Janet Yellen for US Treasury Secretary

Land of Plenty—Plenty of Systems

NOVEMBER 9, 2020

TYSON GREER

We, in America, take so much for granted. We're a First World country. We expect streetlights to come on at dusk and traffic lights to change from red to green. (In Seattle, we even expect people not to jaywalk.)

We expect garbage pick-up on Thursdays, grocery stores to be open seven days a week, Amazon Prime to deliver in a day, and on Saturday nights or a full moon, a longer wait time in a hospital Emergency Department. The service systems that support our lives form a comfortable kind of background noise.

One thing that the pandemic has exposed is the fragility of our systems.

This month I'll attain the age of "double 7" and, in my lifetime, there has never been a time when grocery store shelves were empty or when hospitals beds were full.

Sure, when wind-whipped newscasters warn us of (another) "storm of the century," there is a run on plywood, plastic sheeting, staple guns, batteries, and water bottles. But that's local. It could be Florida and Alabama, then maybe Georgia and South Carolina, but the pandemic situation created a storm of buying food staples in every single state.

Thinking of our food pipeline, our lifeline, as frail is new and frightening. We've always assumed that the sight of 12 different kinds of non-dairy milk and 43 different types of hot sauce was as dependable as Mount Rainier—forgetting that our mountain, snow-shouldered and serene, is in an earthquake zone and predicted to go off magnificently sometime within the next 300 years, more or less.

Panic-buying stripped grocery shelves of basics we take for granted like flour, yeast, canned goods, and toilet paper; and created new markets for hand sanitizer, which also became unavailable last spring. Our local hardware store got a pallet of gallon-sized bottles of alcohol and quart-sized bottles of aloe vera and printed the "recipe" for making your own.

Typically, active dry yeast sales peak in November and December with holiday baking and slump in the first quarter of the year. But demand swelled in Spring and the yeast supply chain can't activate itself. Suppliers of jars and paper packages couldn't meet demand, which led to the Great Yeast Shortage of 2020.

When restrictions shut down restaurants, millions of people remembered the joy of cooking and snapped up pasta and rice like there was no tomorrow. Actually, like they knew there was going to be a very different tomorrow, and the day after, and the day after.

"Farm-to-table" is a catchy slogan/adjective, but that oversimplifies the complex web that makes up our food supply system. It doesn't acknowledge the

125

meat packers, who work on assembly lines designed before safe distancing—and died because of the lack of it. It doesn't recognize the 2.5 million farm-workers, mostly Latino, who work in crowded conditions, carpool to work, and subsist in crowded homes. Many "essential workers" can't afford to stay home when they're sick. They walk a tightrope between protecting their health and holding on to their jobs.

The very thought of a physician's practice or a hospital—much less all healthcare facilities in an area—being overwhelmed used to be unthinkable, but now we know what it's like. Reports of patients stored on gurneys in hall-ways made the news, shockingly because it was US news.

It made sense that elective surgeries were postponed, to avoid unnecessary risk to patients, but also to help ensure enough hospital beds and staff to deal with COVID patients. It's one thing to retrofit a garage or a tent in a parking lot into a field hospital—and there finally seems to be enough PPE (personal protective equipment) to go around, although the delays were unconscionable. But nurses, doctors, and medical techs are exhausted from months and months of front-line fighting to save lives. Ironically, the human factor—the heroes we rely on—is the weak link in expanding the chain of quality healthcare. The time it takes now for health workers to disinfect a treatment room means there is less time to see fewer patients in a day.

We experienced this new reality up close and personal. When an onset of excruciating back pain finally drove Jim to see his doctor, he couldn't get an appointment for five days and so they suggested the ER, then another five-day wait to see a specialist, and another ER visit for more tests, and another four days to see another specialist, and finally(!) Jim's suspicion—It feels like my back is broken—was verified.

It makes sense during a pandemic that only the person in need of medical care be allowed into a hospital or doctor's office, but it's tough to do it alone—so much to remember and remember to ask. We figured a work-around: when the doctor enters the room to deliver a diagnosis or treatment advice, Jim calls my cell so I can be "in the room" to ask questions.

Now's the time to sing another chorus of: "It's a First World after all."

As this year rolls to an end, we can still shop for groceries Sunday to Sunday (in person or Instacart), Amazon Prime can still deliver some things in two hours, the shelves of hot sauce are still full, and, as far as I know, no one has been turned away from a hospital. Yet. But Idaho did send some of their patients to Washington State and the COVID numbers keep rising.

We can hope that this pandemic of the century will not fall into the pattern of "storm(s) of the century." By the time another virulent outbreak occurs, or Mount Rainier blows her pretty top, will we know better how to respond to protect lives and livelihoods, and the systems on which we all depend?

Voter Fraud

NOVEMBER 17, 2020

LAURA CELISE LIPPMAN

Yes it happened.
I know.
My sister called;

My crazy cousin
got his Orthodox lackey
to get my aged, tranked uncle
to check the box
for Trump.

He was a card-carrying Dem
now demented
but he did avoid
Abscam conviction
by a hair's breadth
and was involved
in real estate.

Unk said he knew Fred T
who made Donald
fetch his papers
and told him that his son
wasn't going anywhere
'cuz he couldn't keep his
hands off women's pussies

Musings on a Solo Thanksgiving

NOVEMBER 26, 2020

MARY ANN GONZALES

My first thought when I awoke was "I don't have to cook a turkey." My second thought was "I don't GET to cook a turkey."

As we all know cooking a turkey is a big job, but what I remembered was that when it was done, it was a family ritual that I looked forward to.

After the stuffed bird was in the oven the mess cleaned up and the family began to arrive, it became a "project."

Someone would help pull the heavy pan out to baste and check the doneness. When it was declared "perfect," the team clicked into overdrive.

1. Lift the bird onto the platter
2. Drain the drippings into a pan
3. Sharpen the knives
4. Give a lesson making gravy
5. Carve the turkey while teaching the carving skill to another grandson.

Of course, in my small kitchen the potatoes are being mashed, the side dishes warmed or prepared. CHAOS! FABULOUS! A family tradition I will not have today. A great loss.

What I do have is a series of e-mails from the family wishing all a Happppy T. Day while documenting their lives, and calls from other relatives to send wishes.

My call is to my brother who has COVID. He is in Portland and hopefully on the mend. So, I alternately have interactions that are sweet and scary/hopeful.

Thanksgiving Day is really just another day—one in which we have assigned certain rituals, but ultimately a day to count blessings. I am counting mine. In the time of COVID this takes on another hue. Being solo on this day is mildly shocking and yet chosen. I am thankful that all my family and friends are being smart about protecting themselves wearing those annoying, helpful masks and using our "pods" to live safely. My expectation of them is to "Follow the Science."

Grandson Henry arrived with a pumpkin pie. Sweet-smart Henry and I went for a walk to the bluff and talked about many things: back country skiing, job opportunities, the state of change in this COVID world, isolation, joblessness.

When we got home I told him about the Air Fryer I found. Would he like it? No, he says. I tell him it needs a rack. Henry pulls out his phone and orders the rack which will arrive in a couple of days. This ordering things is a world I do not yet know how to manage. He tells me that his dinner tonight will be Lobster with Macaroni and Cheese. YUM. When he leaves, I cook Mac and Cheese for myself. Comfort Food!

Then, at the end of the day that I am "managing," I get news my sister-in-law has cancer. OMG What Next! The health issues of our aging cohort are catching up. I try to put it aside and will climb into bed to watch yet another Christmas movie—predictable enough to lull me to sleep.

So, at the end of the day I am physically healthy, sad, and bored, but so privileged in all ways. The pleasures and sorrows are mixed.

Celebrating in COVID's Shadow

NOVEMBER 29, 2020

TYSON GREER

I always regarded my November 22nd birthday as a holiday, perhaps because every seven years it falls on Thanksgiving. When I was seven, I imagined people across the then-United States sitting down for turkey on my birthday.

This year, my B-day started with a round of languorous phone calls with my L.A. and S.C. family. Later, the grand-twins and their parents arrived bearing poinsettias and moved heavy stuff under cover for the winter, then we gathered safely distanced around our cozy fire pit for Jim's famous cocoa and a B-day celebration on the patio, our outside "room." The whole day—the phone calls and the in-person visit—was perfect because it was so precious to be in touch in any way we could.

As for Turkey Day, Jim and I had the foresight to cancel that back in August. Too risky to do otherwise. We'd made a pact in March: no one comes inside. So, this year was a chance to re-think holiday gatherings. Now, I'm all for tradition. I cannot imagine NOT making gingerbread cookies for Christmas, birthdays; heck, any gathering deserves gingerbread boys, cars, stars, horses, snowmen, dinosaurs, goats, moose, palm trees. My cookie cutter collection from my grandmother is truly impressive. And I like cooking a turkey.

So T-day started with a leisurely round-robin of family phone calls, then it was Jim and me and a 12-pound, 13-ounce slow-roasted turkey (I vacuum sealed most of it for the freezer), sweet potatoes, roasted Brussel sprouts with a splash of balsamic vinegar, my cranberry sauce, sauerkraut (Whoa! Don't turn your nose up if you haven't tried this Baltimore tradition), and my maple-syruped pumpkin pie.

To be honest, the opportunity NOT to worry about who was allergic to which dishes, how deep is the snow on the pass, how late would so-and-so be, and who had to leave early because of thus-and-such was rather liberating.

Then came the surprise phone call from Erik. "We've got our deck set up warm and safe, tested it last night. Would you and Jim like to come over for pie around five?"

On their covered deck, with a windscreen along the railing, a rug on the floor, and tabletop propane heaters, we were oh so comfortable. Then, they presented us with fleecy blankets warm from the dryer! They truly raised the bar by combining Scandinavian "hygge," cozy and comfy, with "friluftsliv," open-air living.

Oh, and pie—Luia baked pumpkin pie, apple pie, and pecan pie.

Imagine choosing vanilla ice cream or whipped cream. Erik served decaf coffee with a splash of Baileys. (Just pause, inhale, and savor all that.) And on the brightly lit deck in the gathering dark (masks on, except when eating), we all had a lot to be thankful for.

So, what is really important? and what is routine? The point is savoring experiences and connecting—connecting with people you love, not replicating the illustration in the March 6, 1943, *Saturday Evening Post*—and saying, "I love you."

We wish you a quiet and healthy Christmas.

DECEMBER 2020

DEC 2: US Attorney General William Barr says there is no evidence of widespread voter fraud in the 2020 presidential election, despite claims by President Trump

DEC 2: The UK becomes the first western country to authorize the Pfizer/BioNTech vaccine for COVID-19

DEC 2: US records its largest daily death toll for COVID-19 at 2,885 and for the first time patient numbers in hospitals exceed 100,000

DEC 3: Dr. Robert Redfield, head of US CDC said about the months ahead, "I actually believe they're going to be the most difficult time in the public health history of this nation."

DEC 4: Presidents Obama, Bush and Clinton said they would be vaccinated against COVID-19 on camera to gain public trust

DEC 5: Russia begins vaccinating people with its Sputnik B vaccine in Moscow, despite the fact that the clinical trials are not completed

DEC 14: US Electoral College electors cast their votes for president and vice president

DEC 21: Jupiter and Saturn achieve the closest great conjunction since 1623 and appear as a single star

DEC 23: President of the Senate (Vice President Mike Pence) receives the electoral vote certificates

DEC 27: US Transportation Security Administration (TSA) reports a new record of almost 1.3 million travelers in US airports, surpassing the record of almost 1.2 million people on December 23

DEC 31: US has 19.5 million COVID-19 cases and 339,000 deaths from the virus (Johns Hopkins University)

Breathe

DECEMBER 9, 2020

WANDA HERNDON

I cannot breathe, sinking into fear.

I am confused and do not understand.
Uncertainty constricts my lungs
and imprisons my breath inside me.
I am afraid.

Am I a witness to my death?
If I do not push against these Kevlar bars, I will die.
I pray for rescue from a dreadful killer of dreams
before life is sucked out of me.

But I am not alone, and feel the power of many
infuse my body with new strength.
We lock arms against a force
of evil that threatens our existence.

Millions protect me, help me survive
as we gasp for air to save us.
Together, we struggle to wrest stolen breath away
from the Amoral Monster compressing our chests.

We battle this Abomination of Humanity
for our souls and our lives.
No white flags in our hands that
satisfy the Obliterator's thirst for pain.

Unafraid, we inhale, exhale, and breathe hope.

Crisis in COVID-time

DECEMBER 10, 2020

TYSON GREER

At 1:09 p.m., Thursday, when we got a text from daughter-in-law Tobi, Jim was fueling up the Subaru. We had been joking about how many months it had been since the last time we were at a gas station.

She wrote:

"Emergency Ohno going to er"

and

"911 911 this is bad medics st house i did cpr."

Called Tobi. Tried to calm her. We drove home quick. Shoved underwear and socks in a backpack, drove to Tacoma, normally an hour away. Traffic was terrible. Minutes dragged as our heartbeats speeded up.

Two days prior, John had had minor surgery, and was recuperating at their home in Tacoma. Then he had breathing difficulties, stopped breathing, unconscious, CPR, EMTs, intubation, transport; and as we barreled down I-5, Emergency Room experts worked to save his life.

We knew even before we got there, we couldn't *see* John.

Hospital parking lot. I went to the first checkpoint, had my forehead temperature "wanded," and answered "no" truthfully to the list of symptom questions. "Why..." I didn't say... "Why check my temperature if a person is COVID-contagious three to five days before a temperature and if 40% of people with COVID are asymptomatic?"

COVID time. New rules: One family member a day, same person, no "swapping out" privileges. I wouldn't be able to even give Tobi a well-needed respite. Back to the car. Jim paid for the valet parking, the only option, and received the ticket in exchange for his keys.

Until his COVID test results were in, Tobi couldn't see him either. She sat in the waiting room, then was invited to wait in the family room. The chaplain was very attentive to her, and even came outside and talked to us. Very nice man. The parking attendants abruptly returned Jim's keys and his credit card without running it.

Waiting and texting. Later she learned the reason the chaplain had been so attentive was because he'd been alerted that John wasn't expected to make it. The role of the chaplain is an invisible extension of nursing triage: who of those waiting will soon need the most? The parking attendants were in on it.

We sat in the car, twenty-five feet from the hospital entrance for three hours. Waiting and texting.

The shadows from the building and spindly trees crept across the parking lot. Jim and I watched a steady trickle of people go in and out of the hospital.

When there was more than one, they waited six feet apart. Most people wore masks or were given them inside. Most wore them too loosely. That drove me crazy. Occasionally, someone walked out with purpose in their step, shepherding someone released from hospital. That made me envious.

Sometime after five p.m. Tobi took a break from her vigil and came out to talk to us. I didn't recognize her.

Grief and fear changes people. So hard not to fold her in my arms. So cruel to console at arm's length. The six-foot gulf of physical distance is an ocean of sadness. With our love wrapped around her, Tobi went back inside to wait. She still couldn't see him. John had been isolated in the COVID ICU unit, just in case. Later we found out that they didn't move him because the risk was too great.

Jim and I busied ourselves getting something to eat and finding a hotel.

Five thirty p.m. on Thursday, a weekday, few downtown restaurants were open. Lots of large Black Lives Matter signs on the deserted main street. Near-empty light rail cars silently slipped by. We passed Zeek's Pizza; drove on. Around the block, found a wood-fired pizza place. I masked up, went inside to order take-out, but the entrance to the bar-pizza place seemed dark, tight, constricted, and some tables were filled with laughter. Back to Zeek's. The only diners, a father-daughter twosome sitting at a table, looked up and the little girl smiled as we came in, ordered behind the Plexiglas barrier, went back outside to wait.

Found the hotel we'd stayed in before. Small comfort in the familiar. The masked-up man at the front desk and I struggled to hear each other and leaned around the Plexiglas. Touched elevator buttons with our elbows. Opened the door to 432 and washed our hands. Urgent call to front desk: "I need a bottle of sanitizer." A skinny, young man knocked and held a bottle of hand sanitizer at arm's length. I should have said "spray bottle." He came back and I sprayed everything but Jim.

At 11:35 p.m., Tobi called, relief swelling in her voice: the COVID test was negative.

At 2:23 a.m., I remembered a conversation Jim and I had a few weeks ago: "If we're ever in a hotel room during COVID-time, we'll turn off the room air circulation and open a window. Preferably we'd have a room with a fireplace and use that for heat." I opened the window and let city night air in. It wasn't that cold. I checked my phone, too.

Friday morning, sometime after 5 a.m. Tobi called. Visiting hours had begun and, sans sleep, she was there. Room 5a2 in the COVID unit was small. "Imagine a regular ICU room, then divide it in half, and fill half of it with equipment," she said. The area had been retrofitted to handle eight supremely contagious cases and the pace was the same as an ER unit. Staff wore hazmat suits fighting for the lives of the four COVID patients. The rooms were under negative pressure, glass doors swishing shut or open to prevent contaminated air from escaping. Tobi was terrified. We were thankful John didn't have COVID, and we were terrified.

We're grateful for Tobi's long, long, long, days-long stream of texting with us—so many back-and-forth texts that if we earned $ for each text, we could not only surpass the GDP of a developing country, we could probably buy it.

My cell phone now sleeps next to me. Sometimes the notification beeps wake me up—I think about the beeps and dings of the equipment that must crowd John's room—but these are about buses re-routed due to a "civil disturbance" downtown, or urgent pleas to donate to a candidate in any one of a dozen states before the matching deadline. Sleep is a fickle friend.

I decide to keep a notebook. All notes in one place. Good idea. Even so, Friday, Saturday, Sunday, and Monday are now a blur. Always breathlessly awaiting the texts and phone catch-up calls with Tobi, and hearing the results of tests, tests, more tests. Jim and I huddled together over Tobi's voice coming through the tiny cellphone speaker. And the phone calls with his far away kids, wanting to come, persuading them not to.

During these days, the focus shifted from "Will he live?" to "Can he breathe on his own?" Not yet? His vitals are looking good. Next day, "Can he breathe on his own?" Not yet sure. Consequences of long intubation are well documented.

The darkest time was Tuesday morning. The night before, we learned they planned to remove the ventilator early in the morning. At 5:36 a.m. Tobi texted that John had become extremely agitated. Then the phone went quiet. No texts. Seven o'clock. Eight. Nine. Ten. Tried to think "no news is good news...." Failed at that. We held each other.

The cell phone has been our lifeline to John—hearing from Tobi how he was, how horrific it was, and staying strong for her, our soldier on the front line. That one degree of separation alternately seemed a thousand miles away and breathlessly close to the uncertainty that bred fear.

We imagined at some point, what it would have been like trying to keep in touch if a pandemic occurred thirty years ago, without mobile phones—when we couldn't have texted with John's children spread out across Montana, Oregon, and Hawaii. And all desperate to come. Not to mention brothers in Oregon and Auburn. As it was, we were hungry for the information Tobi fed us, and we fed the family through group text several times a day, treading that fine trustworthy line between scary detail and Pollyanna. No lies, no "tomorrow they'll try..." expectations.

Progress, people say, is two steps forward, one step back. Makes it sound like a dance step you know how to do. But you hang on every word in every text, and try to tease the meaning out of every inflection in a phone call.

And all the time, the shadow of COVID looms. Tobi going into the hospital, and out of the hospital. Risk knows no boundaries. "What if *she*..."

The reconfigured space for the COVID Unit is safe, Tobi tells us—the most protective air filtration system, all the sanitizing and separation you could ask for. But sound still travels.

COVID time. New rules: At "end of life," the family is allowed to gather outside the room of the dying patient. Tobi calls us and relays John's agitation at hearing the wails of the family outside the room next door. They're clustered close, looking through the glass door, wailing. In our mind's eye, we see them and feel for them. Jim tells her to play the audio tapes of the Canoe Journey song and his brother James's medicine song for John. She turns them up loud to shield him from the requiem of death. The drumming vibrates on a cellular level.

It's been a week. Each time I wake up, anxiety thrums as I check if there's a new text from Tobi. John's numbers improve. Infection abates. One by one, they remove his life-saving drugs, his tubes, his IV. They find a bed and he's transferred from the frantic pace of the ICU to a private room. The healing—the long, long, long journey of healing—begins. And we are grateful down to our bones.

Kindness in Crisis

DECEMBER 10, 2020

SUZANNE TEDESKO

We've all heard the old saying that nothing brings people together like a crisis. Kindness and generosity generally flourish as people unite against a common enemy. Be it an attack on Pearl Harbor or an act of nature like an earthquake, hurricane, fire or flood, individuals summon up their best selves. At least initially. The COVID-19 pandemic is no exception.

When President Roosevelt declared war on Japan before a joint session of Congress, Senators and Congressional representatives who'd stood miles apart politically—some diehard isolationists—gave their unwavering support.

I've witnessed this flush of instant community a number of times. As a college freshman, I remember first learning that President Kennedy was shot from a gas station attendant when I stopped to fill up en route to New Haven. After sharing the news, the attendant and I locked eyes and teared up—both of us, a total stranger and I, in our common shock and grief.

We saw it in the immediate aftermath of 9/11 as firefighters from all over the country descended upon New York to help search for survivors and aid with relief efforts. We witnessed it again with the outpouring of citizen support after Hurricane Katrina, and we're seeing it today in the selfless dedication of healthcare providers and other essential workers who put themselves at risk to deliver hands-on services deemed essential to our lives.

Times of crisis require prompt responses on a macro level from national, state, and local officials. In mid-March 2020, President Trump declared a state of emergency and together, Congressional Democrats and Republicans hashed out a relief package for shuttered businesses and furloughed workers. Seattle Mayor Jenny Durkan approved a sixty-day moratorium on residential and commercial evictions, and although schools were shuttered, many districts continued to offer free hot meals to children who otherwise might go hungry.

In addition, many everyday Americans are moved to help in whatever small way they can. The virulence of COVID-19, however, and quarantine restrictions have limited traditional ways of reaching out during a crisis. Volunteering at social service agencies and food banks, providing shelter for displaced persons, offering respite care for those attending the sick and disabled or helping young parents who work remotely with their children at home—all are impossible with quarantine restrictions in place. The desire to help and not being able to, of having no agency, can leave one feeling powerless, cut off and redundant. This has been particularly painful as I watch my own children struggle as two working parents with little ones at home and no daycare.

Nonetheless, despite the constraints of quarantine restrictions, individuals have found creative ways to spread joy and good will. In March, a celebratory wave of communal clapping began in Paris and quickly spread to other cities including Rome, Madrid, Vancouver, BC and on March 26, to Seattle when our Office of Arts and Culture encouraged residents to come out on front porches at 8 pm to clap, holler and cheer for our essential workers. Young children were invited to bang on pots and pans. With parties cancelled and weddings postponed, it was as close to a communal celebration as we could get.

Although people still can no longer gather inside, I count myself privileged to live in a pleasant neighborhood with an abundance of green space where I can breathe fresh air, stretch my legs and commune with nature. On my regular walks, I've witnessed numerous gestures of kindness and generosity as households consider what they can do to help others within the restricted parameters of their lives. Some share food, leaving out bags of apples and crates of vegetables from their garden with "Help Yourself" signs or turn their "Little Libraries" into food pantries.

Others leave out small toys for children. Fairy gardens have sprung up in several yards to delight children, while one home features a front yard "I Spy" treasure hunt with a dozen objects camouflaged but within sight to identify from the sidewalk. Some neighbors employ whimsical touches—masked flamingos in the front yard, shrubs with googly eyes or friendly stuffed animals waving from an inside window—all to lift spirits or draw smiles from passersby. Who can't use a dash of laughter in these trying times? And so, for the first few months of the COVID-19, from February 11 when the virus first got its name, a spirit of good will generally prevailed.

And then, as if by a swipe of the finger, everything changed. The pandemic became politicized.

On April 3, the CDC reversed its earlier advice and recommended that all people wear face coverings in public. When President Trump said he wouldn't wear one, masks became the Maginot Line dividing wearers who followed the science and deniers loyal to President Trump who considered wearing masks a sign of submission. What should have been a moment of national unity fractured as politics suffused public health policy. Soon the pandemic became a furnace for polarization.

About the same time, several state governors, most of them Democrats, issued stay-in-place mandates. The political right cried foul, declaring the lockdown orders an overreach, an infringement on their personal freedom. Thousands marched, maskless, in several state capitals. Some were gun-toting members of armed militia groups; others, white supremacists, carrying Confederate flags. President Trump stoked the protests with inflammatory tweets directed at Democratic governors. In Michigan, where COVID-19 deaths at the time exceeded all other states save for three, Democratic Governor Gretchen Whitmer issued a stringent lockdown order which not only generated protests, but death threats and an actual plot to kidnap and kill the Governor. The country had moved beyond hate speech, blame and vociferous shouting—amplified by the media—to actual plans for domestic terrorism, fueled by, of all things, the pandemic.

Just when one might have hoped the ugliness had reached its apex, police killed a Black man, George Floyd, in an appallingly cruel and senseless murder that was captured on video. The incident, the most recent in a series of police brutality occurrences involving Black men and women, uncovered the extent of smoldering racism that Trump had used to build his base. At the same time, it outraged millions of other Americans of all ages and races, launching an outpouring of support for the Black Lives Matter movement. Massive protests against police brutality and racism erupted in cities around the world. The vast majority of social justice protesters wore masks and social-distanced, contributing little to the spread of the virus despite gathering in large numbers. A handful of violent incidents and property damage tarnished the overwhelmingly peaceful demonstrations, providing grist for a law and order backlash by Trump loyalists.

In the months that followed, election politics dominated the airwaves as a desperate President, seeing his poll numbers drop precipitously, sought to restrict voter registration and prevent efforts to expand state mail-in ballots. For Democrats, mail-in balloting was essential, as in-person voting in crowded polling places was considered risky for those following CDC guidelines. The Trump administration responded by reducing Post Office hours, closing mail sorting sites and planting fears of mail fraud. Anxiety on both sides mounted as the election drew near. Despite contracting the illness himself in October, President Trump aligned with conspiracy theorists in the final weeks before the election, calling the pandemic a hoax—fake news.

Fortunately, the election is finally behind us. Although President Trump still hasn't conceded, he will be leaving office. And a COVID-19 vaccine—in fact, several—are on track for distribution. The pandemic may be over soon but sadly, it will leave behind, as a viral footprint, a nation more divided than before. And while kindness and good will haven't been eradicated, they are in crisis—siloed, as we are, in our own pre-sorted communities of like-minded individuals. PLU's—people like us who share our politics, our values. I still see examples of charity and good will as I walk my West Seattle neighborhood but last week, I set out to walk a purportedly lovely wide trail south of us in a neighborhood where the surging infection rate was twice that of my hood. Surely people on the trail would take social distancing seriously, I thought. Instead, more than half of the people we passed wore no masks. My husband and I scrambled into the bushes on our side of the trail, trying to gain six feet of distance, but the unmasked walkers and runners who approached were oblivious or unconcerned, making no effort to give us space.

Still, come January 20, unless something unimaginable occurs, we will have a new President and VP in the White House. Once we subdue the pandemic, the question will be, can we quell the hatred that infects both sides and agree to disagree without demonizing each other. We'll need to find neutral venues where people can come together to talk and listen with open hearts, without interrupting, moving beyond culture war rhetoric to share our values, our fears, our stories. We need to put away our hatchets and find the tools to build a sense of common purpose and civility across the political divide. Only then will our nation truly earn a clean bill of health.

I Try To Be Grateful

DECEMBER 14, 2020

LAURA CELISE LIPPMAN

I tried to be grateful for my husband this morning.
He's pissed I want the car which I usually cede to him
because he's so A.D.D. and I,
I'm just a little.
I tried to be grateful because I have him
and I know my friend Jane has no one,
she's alone in this pandemic wilderness.
She goes for long walks
with a borrowed dog.
I remind myself I at least
have someone to bicker with
all day long,
unless I let him have the car.
I can stay home and dream
and watch the water rise
and fall with the tide.
I can be thankful the monstrous fir
that floats astride the slack,
that's as long as the ferry,
doesn't hit our bulkhead
and smash our ladder
into ricely bits.
I admit I'm thankful for my neat
warm house
when the sky is grey
and the rain hits the metal roof
like fusillades of bullets.
I try to imagine sunshine and beach time
at Playa del Carmen but awake
from my daydream to my cranky spouse.
He must be tired of my naggy jabs
and my saggy flesh.
I'm thankful he's not my friend's spouse
who has back pain and whose
doctors don't seem to realize he has cancer
unless proven otherwise.
I try hard to remember love,

to be love, to emanate love
instead of nasty.
Maybe tomorrow I won't read the news. I'll radiate sunshine
and elevate all around me
so we can beam down
on those around us
and spread much needed joy.

Not Just Any Day

DECEMBER 14, 2020

TYSON GREER

The day dawned gray, as days in November-December-January-February in the Northwest often do. Gray sky, gray lake. The day was cloaked in a cottony, undifferentiated gray, lacking the usual subtle tonal range of the color.

On this day, the COVID-19 death toll rang hollowly for 300,000 lost lives in the US, still the world leader in deaths from the virus. But that somber fact wasn't all that made this day different. Members of the Electoral College in 50 states rolled up their sleeves and faithfully cast their votes and American healthcare workers rolled up their sleeves and accepted the first shots of the experimental vaccine. The voting affirmed our democracy; the vaccine affirmed the world's capability to unite with deliberate speed against a common enemy.

There will be more difficult days ahead. Rolling out the fragile cold chain of vaccine delivery in the US and around the world is a Herculean task. Finding common ground between the 81,282,896 who voted for Biden-Harris and the 74,222,484 who voted for Trump-Pence feels like a double Herculean task. Our country is politically divided between those relieved and those aggrieved. Both wars are not over.

But today, today is a day like no other.

Reflections on 2020

MARY ANN GONZALES

Every year I write a Christmas letter. It tells about the wonderful, splashy events of my year. This year I sat down with my pencil and nothing came out. However, I began to get glimmers of kindness and love. It was like a little string of fairy lights in my mind.

The bucket of Asian pears, the help with my computer woes, the long distance calls, the legal assistance, the fuzzy bunny with a finger bandage, the pictures of new babies in the family, the Writerly Women that listened, the long e-mails, the packet of almonds, the road trips, the sitting in waiting rooms, the invitations to walk, the Cuban sandwiches, the gifts of yard work and housework, calls every morning, those who brought food and sat on the patio.

I found purpose when it was clear we needed COVID masks and I could make them. I was blessed with family and friends who taught me how, ordered supplies, provided yards and yards of fabric.

I found an outlet for feelings when the plan for a book of essays and poetry *Writing While Masked: Observations on 2020* was launched and I could share my experience of this sequestering.

I found a free air fryer and began a new way to cook.

I found a renewed pleasure in the small things: the sunrise and sunset, the raking of autumn leaves, the sun on my face as I sat on my deck, the cookies from a neighbor.

And now it is time for Christmas. It will be a new experience to not have a house filled with family; no turkey to cook, no grandchildren to hug, no tree with the beloved ornaments.

I am grateful that my family is being wise and not gathering. We are showing our love for each other by the wisdom of staying apart.

TYSON GREER

When a plague swept through London in 1606 and theaters closed, Shakespeare locked down and penned *King Lear, Macbeth*, and *Antony and Cleopatra*.

In 2020, as if a pandemic weren't enough, the conjunction of our country's presidential election, torrent of mis- and dis-information, unparalleled divisiveness, and looming racial reckoning made the year remarkable. But as time goes on, we often forget the little things—the details of an event or a year.

We know now that it was a year ago, December 2019, when COVID-19 first gained a foothold on our shores. We know now that COVID mutates; it adapts. And we have adapted, too.

When frightened shoppers stripped shelves clean of products we've always expected to be available—flour, toilet paper, yeast, sanitizers—we made do and sometimes made jokes. Memes bounced around Facebook advising of the perfect present for any special occasion: a roll of gift-wrapped toilet paper. When consumer shopping stalled, small businesses, always the most nimble, shifted their product lines and produced masks, to stay afloat and to contribute to the fight.

It would have been easier if we had just one front to fight this year. But the virus knocked down our economy, the Tweeter-in-Chief in the White House pinballed lies to an unimaginable level, and the gloves have been thrown off the depth and complexity of our nation's deeply embedded racism.

The word privilege no longer refers to "people who automatically go to the front of the line." Privilege is color-coded. White privilege means you don't have to worry that a policeman will put his knee on your lilywhite neck for eight minutes and look into the camera while you die.

As the mother of two white boys, I never worried about them being stopped by cops for "Driving-while-Black" or "Walking-while-Black," or "Jogging-while-Black" or "Standing-around-while-Black" or...

Racism isn't always about imminent death. I, for one, had no idea that mothers warned their Black daughters and sons to "keep the receipt!" so they could prove, when questioned, that they had paid for the item their Black selves were accused of stealing. Death by a thousand cuts to your sense of your intrinsic value.

Racism runs deep, but fortunately, many good souls in these Dis-united States have adapted their understanding of the cultural norm, which had over-simplified the choices of being "Racist" or "Not-Racist." In truth, you're either for it, or you're actively against it. There is no middle ground on which to stand and claim neutrality.

In the same vein, Democrats who didn't stand up and vote in the 2016 election can thank themselves for four years of the Trump regime's assaults on decency, civility, and our democracy. You're for or against this behavior; I don't see a middle ground. Hence the problem that will remain when the Trump coven relinquishes the White House.

Although in 2020 Trump's response to COVID pedaled backwards and sideways faster than forward, many states and jurisdictions issued directives and sound advice to thwart the virulent advance. We're fortunate in Washington State to have re-elected Jay Inslee, a governor who speaks science (COVID crisis and climate emergency).

Recently, Dr. Anthony Fauci, who emerged as our most trusted health voice, sounded the alarm that December, January, and February will be the darkest days. After seeing the spikes in COVID cases even before counting those from the Thanksgiving holidays, this rings true. On December 2, COVID hospitalizations in the US jumped to 100,000 a day—three times the number on October 1. Seattle's Harborview Medical Center's ICU units are now at 90%

capacity. Experts predict 450,000 US deaths by April 2021. If you want to see the end of this tunnel, do not remove your mask.

To avoid contributing to the statistics, Jim and I continue not inviting anyone inside and ordering groceries online. We're ordering take-out twice a week to help our favorite small restaurants survive. Foodbanks will continue to need us more than ever, as the Senate fiddles lamely.

In the solitude of 2020, our garden has received special attention. Besides the peas, kale, lettuce, beets, tomatoes, onions, strawberries, blueberries, raspberries, and abundance of parsley, we're glad we completed the Great Excavation and Storm Drainpipe Laying Project and are still speaking to each other.

Now in winter, we've adapted cheerfully to "outside-living." Our (hygge and friluftsliv) patio space glows with a fire ring, a tabletop propane heater (early Christmas present), and warm-from-the-dryer blankets.

This morning, the sun lifted above the horizon at 8:07 a.m. into a cloudless sky. We have 14 days until Winter Solstice, when we in the northern latitudes rejoice that each day the sun will rise higher in the sky and lift our spirits with it. On December 21, the image of the Jupiter and Saturn conjunction will serve as a metaphor of hope: those which are separate can come together.

Regarding latitudes, of course it was disappointing not to pal around New Zealand with Beth and Vicki or visit friends in Idaho and Santa Fe, or Aaron and Tori in L.A., or our family in Canada. But if there's one thing I've adapted to this year, it's thinking about empty and full. Empty of expectations and full of possibilities.

Random reflections reflect gratitude:

1. Still above ground and happily married
2. Hummingbirds dine at the feeder and watch us eating at the dining room table
3. Zoom yoga freed us from struggling to find a parking place at 8:15 a.m.
4. We learned how to wash our hands properly, not just baptize them
5. The garden never looked better
6. Our daily walks are part of our life now
7. Time to notice and reflect has won over busy, busy, busy
8. I like the similarity between my calendar and the Canadian tundra
9. We've laughed harder at the silliest things
10. I haven't gained weight
11. Our writing group is my metronome
12. Phone time and real time with family and friends is even more precious
13. My second novel is almost finished
14. Breadmaking is as much a rhythm as breathing
15. I like writing essays

Neither I nor anyone in our writing group will claim accomplishments of Shakespeare's measure, but we did write...and write...and write. As this kaleidoscopic year evolved, we wrote as a way to make sense of it all. We wrote to remember this watershed year, and to learn from it what to keep and what to keep from happening again.

WANDA HERNDON

Things will get better!

Yes, for sure! I will always remember 2020 as the year of lies, videotape, more lies and possible recovery for many people stricken with ignorance, mental illness, physical impairments, or depression...remnants from the assault on all of our senses. The avalanche of misinformation about COVID-19: everything from the invisible corner we were rounding away from the virus, masks do not prevent transmission of germs, and the big one: Donald Trump defeated Joe Biden in the 2020 US Presidential election. Every sane person (I pride myself in being one of them) in the world knows that this is "crazy talk."

So, 2020 was a year during which we fought until we almost reached the limits of our ability to resist and then we fought some more. Our pending reward: the truth, which will soon set us free when President-elect Joe Biden and Vice President-elect Kamala Harris are sworn into office on January 20, 2021. I remind myself that this day is really just around a real corner, and all I have to do is just hang on and things will get better!

Over the last four years, I have ranted and raved about the incompetence, cruelty, thievery, criminality, hatefulness, discrimination, and other despicable behaviors of the amoral leaders who have occupied our highest public offices.

This is why I was almost brought to tears of relief and joy when two decent, moral, competent, history-making leaders, Joe and Kamala, as we affectionately refer to them, were named the apparent winners of the 2020 US presidential election. My faith in the goodness of our citizens has been reaffirmed and I believe I can actually see the elusive corner that we are rounding. It leads to freedom from a diabolical band, who committed awful acts against humanity and perpetrated their bad intentions on everyone who was different from them. But now, we, the people, have cut the legs from their hideous torsos on which they stood looking down on decent people. Daily news reports document their tumbling falls from whence they came, and I look forward to when they reach their hell-ish destination in one huge splat.

However, during their four-year reign of terror, I refused to be beaten into submission and pushed forward with life, such as it was. When I flew home to Seattle from California on Wednesday, March 4, 2020, after attending the beautiful wedding of my friends, Mary Williams and Pat Gallis, I did not realize that this was the only trip I would take this year. Since my calendar was booked with various trips to exotic locations in the world, I never thought that my wings would be clipped, and I would be earthbound until who knows when.

COVID-19 forced all of us to view the world through a new lens that required innovation. I am blessed with the ability to entertain myself and I am grateful that I was able to fill my time with more Zoom meetings/happy hours/ check-ins than I can count with family and friends; my writing group; Greater Seattle Chapter of The Links, Inc. meetings; Alpha Kappa Alpha Sorority (Kamala's sorority as well) events; socially distanced walks with the ladies who comprise the Seattle Thursday Walkers, who actually walk Monday through Friday; W Communications business meetings; and other activities appropriate for a lock-down lifestyle.

Of course, I cannot forget the joy I received from hours and hours of streaming some of the best shows on broadcast television and streaming channels. I am not ashamed to admit that I often built my entire day around the next episode of my favorite television series that I usually watched while lounging on my sofa! Luckily, I did not eat myself into a stupor and was able to maintain my weight loss thanks to Weight Watchers.

As I sought to fill my time with meaningful, interesting activities, I was surprised that my creativity, once dormant, broke out of my politically obsessed, locked-down brain to work on my memoir, *Dreadlocks in the Boardroom*; write poetry, one poem, "I Cry," was published in the *Seattle Times* on June 13, 2020, and is included in this book; and draft and deliver motivational talks for various virtual conferences.

And I refused to allow COVID-19 to take my joy as I virtually celebrated birthdays of family members and friends, weddings and the lives of loved ones who passed during this time.

I pray 2020 was an anomaly and that the promised vaccine will save lives and release us 100 percent from virus purgatory. However, I would be naïve to believe that life before COVID will return. It cannot.

I understand that we cannot allow ourselves to be lulled into pre-COVID states of euphoria, longed for in my quiet moments. I accept that the foundation for more health-conscious years to come has been laid. And this is fine with me.

As Celie in *The Color Purple* film said and I quote in gratitude, "...dear God, I'm here." And my belief in our world is as strong today as it was yesterday and getting stronger.

I know it will get better!

LAURA CELISE LIPPMAN

It seemed like background chatter about our unhinged narcissistic leader has been with us constantly for the last three years. 2020 brought with it the hope of a new election and replacement of the Maniac-in-Chief. My people and I were all terrified the nightmare of the past three years would continue should he not be defeated. The idea of electing a new charismatic progressive leader gave us hope. For all of this year, new sensationalistic headlines rewarded our self-destructive "doom-scrolling" habit that took up too much of each day.

On the family front, I was looking forward to a new baby; my daughter was just pregnant with her second baby and maybe the fourth grandchild in the family would be a girl!

Then we got hit with the VIRUS. The newly identified coronavirus, which upended everything.

The lockdown. Never had we experienced such a thing. Although epidemics/pandemics underscore human history, because of a combination of effective vaccinations, medical advances, and sheer luck, large cohorts of western civilization had not been struck down during my lifetime as they had been in previous epochs. Most of us were lucky enough to avoid being affected by AIDS, N1H1, Zika and before that scarlet fever, polio and TB. This time we might not miss out. Whether or not we became physically ill, everyone in our country has been affected by the new virus. Our governor in Washington state was the first official in the country to declare a lockdown. Life has not been the same since. First we had to figure out where it was safe to go. The grocery store? Pharmacy? Hardware store? We were stuck inside except for WALKS!

The mayor of Seattle closed our major parks to avoid people using them as meeting places outside their homes. Playground equipment was off limits for the grandchildren, because no one knew if the virus could be transmitted from surfaces. What was the correct/safe etiquette regarding checking produce for ripeness in the markets?

First we wore gloves, then we found out that fomite transmission risk was small.

There was the PPE fiasco. We received mixed messages about wearing surgical masks...to wear or not to wear? Would we deny our health care workers the limited availability of these precious resources? The federal government, denying the importance of this outbreak, was unwilling to provide leadership in manufacture and distribution of crucial supplies. We've watched the science and the mores change over the course of this year. Our president suggested unproven therapies and even suggested injecting bleach into our bodies. The unexpected consequences of those suggestions were truly hilarious send-offs; Sarah Cooper and Steve Colbert delivered some of my favorites. Now of course, we can't leave the house without our mask. I haven't settled on which style/fabric is most comfortable. A year ago, this question would not even have been imaginable.

Watching the nightly news brought new interest: suddenly we could peer into the homes of the reporters and anchors; check out their pets, their furnishings and especially the contents of their bookshelves. It was fascinating that most of the "backdrops" became more tidy and staged over the course of this year. There must be a new business in video background consulting for TV anchors, correspondents and contributors!

Our president and his relentless assault/sidelining of public health is a spectacle for the ages, horrifying, but familiar. This is not the first time a leader has ignored public health measures to better his or his party's own fortunes. I found bookending the year with the great courses series by Dorsey Armstrong, *The Black Death: The World's Most Devastating Plague,* and *The Great Influenza* by John M. Barry most useful for giving me perspective on this unusual and unbalancing time.

I look around my house and wonder why I care what it looks like if only my husband and I see it? Meanwhile, we, along with our family and friends, created an outdoor entertainment area, with lights and outdoor heaters for outdoor visiting when the weather permits.

My daughter's pregnancy progressed; first we worried about possible cytokine storm in pregnant women, during the pregnancy and then at delivery, then, possible vulnerability of the newborn concerned us. When it was all over and done with, a healthy baby girl produced (a Pandemic Baby), we learned that yet again the people at greatest risk are the "elderly" grandparents. All of a sudden I became high risk; me, the mountain climber, adventurer, hiker extraordinaire was reduced to liability. How a year can change one's perception of oneself!

At first we could be in a "pod" with our grandchildren and their parents— help provide some daycare even. But as the months passed, the difficulties of my children working and doing their own daycare within the confines of their own houses became too difficult. Plans changed, as the daycares/preschools reopened, their kids went back to school after months of toddler Zoom calls.

In person schooling has been much better for the kids and the parents, but in spite of mask wearing, spacing in classrooms and lower numbers of children in each room, it was too much of a risk to expose them indoors to us, the grandparents. My husband and I see them outdoors. At least the play structures and parking lots in the parks are now accessible. Mostly however, we walk to the parks, because we can't be in the same vehicles with the children.

Our Family dinners inside—a weekly highlight long banished.

Zoom, now an activity, became an integral part of our lives. I just attended my second Zoom memorial service, and it did have its advantages. All the attendees were named on the screen, and I could attend a service for a person who died 3000 miles away from me. I could see her nieces, nephews and children and see the faces of the deceased and her long dead husband, close family friends, reflected in all the friendly countenances.

We have watched our leader systematically undo climate change protections. It has been heart-breaking. We can only hope that much of his evil can be undone. The polar ice caps are melting, the oceans are rising, the earth's temperature has been the highest ever recorded in the last two years, the Western USA and Australia have been ravaged by wildfires, and yet the climate change deniers persist in believing people have not contributed to these changes. I wonder that their pocketbooks seem more important than their grandchildren.

Speaking of leaders; there is light at the end of the tunnel. We have administration change nigh, and our first female, multiracial vice president. KAMALA! and Joe Biden are beacons of hope for a better 2021. We also have hopes of a successful vaccine.

JANE SPALDING

In a "normal" year I would be planning a holiday brunch about now. For the past 22 years, friends and family knew my house was open to all on Christmas morning. Sadly, this year is different. Today Washington's governor extended sweeping COVID-19 restrictions until January 4. There will be no indoor holiday gatherings unless all participants have quarantined for two weeks and tested negative for the virus.

And yet, against the backdrop of all that happened in 2020—terrifying Trumpian tactics, a global pandemic, racial upheaval in this country and the world, fires, and other natural disasters, I have a love story to tell.

Would this love be part of my 2020 story if not for the pandemic? Maybe not. I took a leap of faith when I moved into Nick's home on Whidbey Island to isolate in late March. The shelter-in-place mandate forced togetherness, like Christmas paper whites, to bloom, or not, in a bowl.

What is amazing to me is that gradually two "I's" became a "we." At first, I was the visitor from Seattle staying in his house while waiting for the virus to go away. By the end of August, after a lengthy emotional downsizing process, Nick's daughter, husband and three children moved into his home. He and I settled into my urban one for the months of September and October.

Nick, ever the island boy, had agreed to sub-let the beach home of friends who live in Langley from November till March. "It'll be an adventure," he said. "We'll have time to decide what we want to do next. How we want to live. You'll get to experience what it's like to live on a different part of the island."

Now, in December, the second month of this newest phase of living together, I assure you that winter on Whidbey Island is dark, wet, and cold. Blessings of nature come in a different light. A pink sky in the morning over the snow-covered Cascade Range we can see from our window. The endlessly diverse crops of mushrooms popping up in the woods. The great blue heron who dines outside our door.

During the past nine months, when we've been left to create our own social connections on Zoom, or the phone, or carefully negotiated gatherings in person; when our spiritual practices and educational diversions were up to us;

when our entertainment was often online, I've been blessed to share decisions with a partner who offers compatible companionship.

But what grounds me is that together we've weathered some hard things—finding my beloved daughter struggling with aspects of her life, moving out of the home Nick and his wife shared for fifteen years, living in three different places, and surviving various injuries and aches. A partner you can lean on during crises and transitions is a gift you can't buy. You have to unfold it, layer by layer like the metaphorical onion.

Now, at the end of this year of no normal, I'm surprised at how casually "we" ask people on the island if they know of a house that will be available to rent or to buy. "We"—two seventy-somethings relishing the solid support of four feet on the ground instead of only two.

My new year resolution for 2020 was *give up needing to know what happens next.*

For twelve months it has been my mantra. Maybe I'll keep the same one for 2021.

SUZANNE TEDESKO

2020: Just two weeks after the first known COVID-19 case in the United States was discovered in Snohomish County, Washington, we welcomed a new grandson, Boden. What a joy, and a relief after our daughter's very scary pregnancy. For the first months of the pandemic, we were able to see our daughter's growing family and help by bringing meals and offering some childcare for three-year old Sky.

Sadly, our son and his family moved to Orcas Island in early February. We sorely missed watching their three-month-old son, Shay's development as the San Juan islands closed to all but full-time residents. Fortunately, his three-year-old sister, Dalton, loved to FaceTime and we'd read and chit-chat several times a week.

In March, the White House declared a state of emergency. The community choir I'd joined was put on hold. Just two weeks later, engineers discovered serious cracks in the heavily trafficked West Seattle Bridge that connects our neighborhood to Seattle proper. Just days later, officials closed the bridge for the indefinite future. "Sorry folks." While it was still possible to get to Seattle, it required a circuitous, nerve-wracking drive south through a truck-laden industrial area before heading back north to Seattle. We had no real choice but to hunker down in our new neighborhood.

Apart from our daughter's family and one other couple, we knew no one, though being new to West Seattle had its rewards. The neighborhood offered an abundance of green space to explore on foot. On our walks, my husband and I roamed through acres of wooded parks, along shoreline trails with mountain views and through leafy residential neighborhoods with glorious gardens. Some liken West Seattle's drier microclimate to California: we can boast a 'heritage' palm tree, the tallest in Seattle, in our front yard.

And there was Zoom. I checked in regularly with current friends and reconnected with old ones from high school and college days. I also participated in online Pilates, yoga and fitness classes and met weekly with the writing group.

Still, four pillars of my past life—travel, refugee work, singing in a choir and political action—were now closed to me. The Grand Canyon river trip I'd planned with my three college roommates was scotched. I realized how much I've relied on travel and the excitement of discovering new places to keep me energized, learning and growing. Without external stimulation, I needed to build inner resources to find meaning while sequestered at home. Writing was key. I am currently finishing a novel and for that, I needed only my wits, motivation and energy. Sometimes, I struggled to muster all three, but once I got going, the challenge of writing fiction galvanized me.

At the end of May, the brutal killing of George Floyd by a Minneapolis police officer shook the nation. Beside myself with rage and grief, I wanted to join Black Lives Matter marches but given my COVID risk level, decided it unwise. I felt powerless. The best I could do was educate myself by reading about systemic racism, and write postcards urging people to vote. Lots of them. Who knows whether they changed anyone's mind, but they helped me feel less impotent.

Thankfully, a windfall diversion presented itself. Our West Seattle daughter and son-in-law both returned to work, virtually. How would they manage with an infant and three-year-old at home? My husband and I jumped in to offer three days a week of "Skyschool." It couldn't have come at a better time. Spending six weeks teaching, playing, crafting, and planting a garden with our grandson was a welcome antidote to the news of the day. In mid-July our son-in-law began seeing patients in person. Because of worry about our risk of secondary exposure, Sky returned to his former preschool. Since then, we only see them masked, outside and 6 feet apart.

By mid-summer, pandemic spread in some areas had dropped off. We could spend time at our Lopez Island cabin and finally, see our Orcas Island family, outdoors. We began to meet a few friends, observing strict protocols. Our peak experiences of the summer both took place on peaks—camping at Mount Rainier with friends from the East Coast and meeting up with our full moon posse for the annual full moon campout on a high ridge in the Olympic Mountains.

Fall brought the expected cool weather and a dangerous pandemic surge. Election drama fraught with mis-information, lies, and attempted voter suppression added to the gloom. To reduce our anxiety, we limited our consumption of news.

The election is finally over and come January, we'll have a new president and a dynamic female vice president. Two new vaccines are nearly ready for distribution. Hallelujah!

I come away from the year with several "ahas." The first, a keen awareness of my mortality. The virus pierced my years of denial and I finally had to admit I'm not forever young. With the spotlight on mortality came a sense of the preciousness of time, of the now. That and gratitude for my health, the privilege of a comfortable home, food on the table and freedom from worry about the rent. Heightened awe at the splendor of nature, and an expanded appreciation for my husband—our closeness and mutual support. And finally, the paramount importance of savoring and holding tight the threads of connection with people dear to me.

As the year draws to a close, I surprise myself with how full my days are. Not so much with home projects or preparing elaborate meals like many friends, but with writing, daily walks, exercise, reading, listening to audiobooks, keeping in touch with friends, streaming good movies and series (as well as media junk food on dark days when I've needed it).

Did I mention that I'm learning to play the ukulele? And with any luck, I'll soon be able to hug and hang with my family again. That day can't come soon enough.

BETH WEIR

On March 14, 2020, I wrote about the creeping awareness of the pandemic, ending it with a quote by the novelist, Gail Sheehy.

"To be tested is good. The challenged life may be the best therapist."

To this I added with naive assurance that 2020 would be an interesting year.

In retrospect, "interesting" was a poor word choice since it has a rational component and 2020 was a long way from rational. "Interesting" as a descriptor was supplanted by bare-knuckled words: angry, embarrassed, incensed, enraged, aggravated, and also fearful come to mind.

2020 has been a hot year for emotions because collectively we have had to keep bobbing up for air. Four waves engulfed us: COVID-19, civil unrest, partisan politics, and severe climate warming events. (Overactive fire and hurricane seasons.)

In the fall, the presidential elections came on top of the "waves." By then we were Zoomed out, chastened by a new understanding of systemic racism and exhausted by Trump's behavior.

The presidential campaign felt like the catastasis of a Greek tragedy. This is the heightened action immediately before the catastrophe unfolds. The President's flouting of scientific advice regarding behavior in a pandemic and his torrent of lies while seeking a return to the White House, was the catastasis. The catastrophe is the tattered state of American democracy that the election and its tortured aftermath underlined. It is going to take a long time before the contempt of the moment will be overtaken by more benign reactions.

As a people we were surely tested, and it didn't end resoundingly well. Sheehy's claim that "the challenged life was the best therapist" was a reach—at least as a nation. The total public experience of 2020 made us all feel as though the world as we knew it was a mirage and collectively, we have been diminished.

My personal experience in 2020 has been different from the collective one, which in retrospect is not surprising. Building a positive personal experience was the only way to counteract the ongoing angst and sustain a spirit.

As a retired senior with introvert tendencies, I settled early into the unformed days to pursue my hobbies of gardening, writing, and reading, none of which were subject to a deadline. Better yet, and to my delight, I discovered a distinct discipline in myself to keep a focus on a project.

I learned a few things along the way that helped, some of which seemed contradictory. It was better to clean up the messes in the house that living creates to preserve a sense of control but-really-nothing happens if you don't put the dishes in the dishwasher all afternoon. Really. Dirty dishes can be quite liberating.

Patience has never my virtue, but I came to love the slow pace of garden life. I had hours to think about the new beds I am creating. Visits to the garden nurseries became treasure hunts rather than check list runs. Better yet, I was able to feed us from my vegetable garden. While the vegetables we consumed were sometimes deformed they were full of sunshine and lovely.

What I am pleased about is that the Coronavirus pounds landed mostly on the dog. Our frequent walks helped me in that regard but, as the scales attest, not him.

Dare I say the word: Interesting. In retrospect I found the personal experience of 2020 exhausting, despair making, sad, frustrating, and also interesting. All the same I hope I'm not tested in 2020 fashion ever again; I've had enough "therapy." I'm desperate to give my grandchildren a hug and have them read me their bad jokes next to me on the sofa instead of via a screen.

The good that may grow out of this total dislocation is the addressing of societal fissures that were revealed. It is the one comfort.

2021 Postscript

The entries for 2021 are a postscript, a record of our adventures and emotions as we strive to work our way back to normalcy, thanks to vaccinations.

JANUARY-JUNE 2021

JAN 6: Following a Trump-led rally, Congress's certification of Electoral College votes was interrupted when a violent mob of Trump supporters stormed into the Capitol, overwhelming security forces and attempting to overturn the 2020 presidential election

JAN 7: At 3:41 a.m., Congress completed certification of Joe Biden as the 46th US President and Kamala Harris as Vice President

JAN 8: Following calls for impeachment or removal from office, President Trump reverses himself and acknowledges a new administration will take office this month, but does not concede

JAN 8: Twitter permanently suspends President Trump's account "due to the risk of further incitement of violence"

JAN 13: US House of Representatives votes to impeach President Trump, this time for "incitement to insurrection"

JAN 20: President Joe Biden and Vice President Kamala Harris are sworn into office

FEB 13: Senate votes to acquit Trump on impeachment charges

FEB 22: US death toll from COVID-19 surpasses 500,000

MAR 2: Estate of Dr. Seuss announces that six of his books will no longer be published due to racist and offensive imagery.

MAR 11: President Biden signs $1.9 trillion rescue package, to distribute $1,400 stimulus checks to people on file with the IRS

MAR 29: Trial against police office Derek Chauvin for the killing of George Floyd begins

APR 14: Biden announces full US troop withdrawal from Afghanistan by Sept 11

APR 20:	Record number of new COVID-19 cases reported in one week according to WHO: 5.24 million
APR 20:	Police officer Derek Chauvin found guilty of the murder of George Floyd.
MAY 7:	Israel-Palestine crisis escalates with Israeli police invading the al-Aqsa Mosque
MAY 10:	Palestinian groups in Gaza fire rockets at Israeli cities and violence escalates
MAY 13:	CDC mandates no masks indoors for those people who are fully vaccinated and no masks are needed outdoors
MAY 19:	World's largest iceberg (1,667 square miles) calves off ice shelf in Antarctica
MAY 24:	India's official COVID-19 death toll passes 300,000 (probably a vast undercount)
MAY 25:	US CDC says half of all US adults are now fully vaccinated,
MAY 31:	President Joe Biden visits Tulsa, Oklahoma, as it marks the 100-year anniversary of the massacre of hundreds of Black residents by a white mob
JUN 1:	Biden administration suspends oil and gas leases in Arctic National Wildlife Refuge
JUN 15:	US death toll from COVID-19 tops 600,000 (Johns Hopkins), with 65% of adults vaccinated with at least one dose
JUN 15:	NY state Governor Andrew Cuomo announces a "return to life as we know it" lifting all COVID-19 restrictions after the state passes 70% vaccinated with one dose
JUN 17:	President Biden signs into law the Juneteenth National Independence Day Act making June 19 a federal holiday commemorating emancipation
JUN 24:	Residential tower Champlain Towers South collapses at 1:30 am in Surfside, Miami Beach, with 156 people missing or dead
JUN 25:	Former US police officer Derek Chauvin is sentenced to 22 years and six months for the murder of George Floyd in Minneapolis

JUN 27:   Hottest temperature ever recorded in Canada at 46.6° C (116° F) in Lytton, British Columbia (breaks record 2 days later with 49.6° C); town then burns to the ground

JUN 27:   Heat dome envelops the Pacific Northwest with Portland, Oregon posting highest temperature since records began of 112° F (broken the next day)

The New Year

LAURA CELISE LIPPMAN

There was change;
hermit shadows over
new angles of propose.

The old year—
dreamlike—passed so slowly
it left residues of bones,
cancelled breath, and lost aromas.

Spring renewed the year
with shoots and shots
and mask litter on the soil and
in the surf.

Children found ways
to amuse themselves
then old playmates
blossomed in their gardens

Adults found new friends
in unsuspected places
nurtured outside,
over fences,
over the fire alarm
computer hacks
and vodka in the night.

Your Ancestors are Looking for You

BETH WEIR

My husband and I learned in January of 2021 you could feel euphoric and peaceful at the same time. Our euphoria derived from being delivered from a two-week quarantine that allowed us to anticipate three COVID-19 free months in New Zealand and our calmness was a response to the fact we'd left the grinding politics of the pandemic behind. It was akin to the moment the leaf blower is turned off.

Our first destination was Palmerston North, where Bruce and I met and married some fifty years ago. Our immediate plan was to visit family; our secondary one to find members who were not now of the realm. Through study in quarantine of a genealogy report prepared by a cousin, I discovered that my great-grandparents were buried close by and since my great-grandmother Ruku was Māori, this would be an opportune time to explore my Polynesian roots.

Our venture and vision were challenged by some realities. We had the names of the roads in the rural location where they rested but not much else.

We ambled blind along one of the listed roads in our rental car, relishing freedom, the sunshine, the burble of the nearby Rangitikei River, the scenery that inspires and suddenly Bruce braked. To our right was a small, gray church with a graveyard. Great-grandfather was easy to locate, heralded as he is by a large, white headstone that seemed at odds in its grandeur with his hardscrabble frontier life.

Now it was time to look for Ruku. Her name is associated with the Tokorangi *Marae*, the sacred gathering place of her tribal people. While we found a road directing us to three different *maraes*, none was Ruku's. Out of options, we took it and at the last *marae* we saw a man examining the carving on the meeting house.

My approach was tentative as it is customary for strangers to be invited onto a *marae* and I did not want to cause offense. When I stated we were looking for the grave of my great-grandmother the man turned his head and asked, "Is her name Ruku Te Kauki?" I nodded yes.

He looked at me then asked, "You must be a Swainson?"

As I nodded again he reeled off the names I had so recently committed to memory of my grandfather and his five siblings born to William and Ruku. While I was standing slack jawed the man pointed to a grand statue carved in the Māori fashion.

"That was Ruku's second husband."

"Henare," I managed to get out.

Now it was the man's turn to nod.

My new friend directed us to Cemetery Hill so we could pay Ruku our respects. On leaving we hugged, and he pressed noses with Bruce in the traditional Māori *hongi*. Surreal is close as an adjective but doesn't quite do the moment justice.

I relayed this story to a Māori acquaintance two weeks later. Ben smiled and said, "Your ancestors are looking for you."

Later Bruce and I returned to revisit the elder we had encountered by chance. This time he took us out to the land Ruku called home and we stood among the tall grasses in the sunshine and admired the great beauty of the landscape that reached to a snowcapped mountain. Suddenly our elder broke into Māori, raised his arms and spoke passionately for five minutes. When finished he explained, "I have given thanks for the abundance of nature and introduced you to your ancestors."

I had another surreal moment that was soon replaced by two emotions I had recently experienced in concert. One was euphoria and the other was peace. I could not have explained them, but they were real.

Eulogy to Democracy in Our Time

LAURA CELISE LIPPMAN

Rattlesnake religions at the altar
of the polymorphous perverse
peopled by blind seers
pursuing gratuitous lucre,
conspiring to end our lovely dream.

A pollution of ideology
fueled by the marriage
of the far right and the super-rich
ends in democracy's demise.

Scheming orthodoxy
coupled with power-mad zealots
invalidate votes
as mobs rage
and bigotry kills suffering suffrage.

Kindness and mercy
are lost on the battlefield;
Jesus' soft femininity
and Quan Yin's tranquil peace
transform and dissolve in acid mists.

Totters, mad plotters, term-extending liars
swarm like scorpions and snakes
onto the rotunda with vulgar display
of Confederate flags,
machine guns and hoisted batons

as our Capitol is breached.
Senators cower in fear
in the building's bowels.
How fast they forget.

Meanwhile the *Cheneys and Bushes* of the world
feign innocence on pretenders' stages
as they allied with preening
scheming *Netanyahus*
and global dictators of the right.

"Defenders of the faithful"
ramblers, dissemblers, bombers of the night
Nazis of the left and right
conspire to sear and ignite
that which we hold dear.

Voices and votes,
those quiet treasures,
well fought,
so easily lost,
now balance at the precipice.

100,000 AND COUNTING

WANDA HERNDON

Who knew that one of my happiest moments would occur at the end of a syringe? This may seem strange, especially to my sisters and brothers who know our country's shameful history of immoral medical treatments and experiments performed on African Americans in the past. The most famous of these is the Tuskegee Study of Untreated Syphilis in the Negro Male (1932-1972).

I was more scared of getting the virus than the shot. However, I never imagined the elation I would feel on February 26, 2021, when I became the 100,000th person to receive the COVID-19 vaccination at Harborview Medical Center in Seattle, WA.

During early 2021, the COVID vaccination dominated my walking group's discussions about current events. Our "maturity" relegated us to the vulnerable group, and we were desperate to be "saved" from this deadly virus.

When I raced out of my new Seattle townhouse on the morning of February 26, leaving moving boxes stacked to the ceiling in every room, I was in a frenzy. I was late picking up my COVID vaccination partner. Our appointments for second shots were 15 minutes apart, and I was determined to get us to the clinic on time, even if I had to run a few red lights.

The timing was tight, but I managed to scoop my friend up from the curb. I gave her a quick once over, processing the fact that she looked like she stepped out of an *Essence* magazine spread and I looked like someone who had been moving boxes for days.

I was a "hot mess": a bright red crumpled, over-sized tee shirt, unruly mane of grey, once blonde hair trapped under a baseball cap, a pair of black leggings, and well-worn tennis shoes completed my "look." This was no time for vanity. I just wanted my "shot" even though negative African American experiences with the medical profession could have discouraged me.

Arriving at our destination, with five minutes to spare, I told my friend to get out so she would make her appointment. She followed my tactless instructions, and miraculously I found street parking.

I signed in...filled out the paperwork and was seated in a nurse's station within 10 minutes of entering the clinic. I was not afraid. In my excitement, I left the completed forms that validated my vaccine eligibility on a table. With adrenaline pumping, I retrieved them and took a few deep breaths.

After I was properly situated, a woman poked her head into my cubicle and asked if I would allow the Harborview Medical media team to interview me about being the 100,000th vaccinee!

A feeling of euphoria spread over me. I let out a yelp and started laughing joyously. I was almost overwhelmed with emotion knowing that I would soon be double vaccinated and therefore safe. There in the tiny stall, the nurse, the media team, and I celebrated this milestone with whoops and hollers.

I did not consider myself camera-ready for an interview—not by the strict standards I set for the media team when I was senior vice president of Starbucks Global Communications.

But I had retired from that life, and I chuckled about breaking my own rules. In this case, the message was more important than how I looked! And the answers to the reporters' questions flowed from my mind to spoken words effortlessly. You would have assumed I'd been prepped as I shared my opinions about why it is important for people, especially people of color, to get vaccinated (https://newsroom.uw.edu/resource/uw-medicine-administers-its-100000th-covid-19-vaccine-dose).

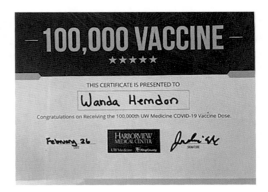

When the interview was over, I proudly cradled my personal vaccine certificate. I hoped that others would follow my example and I gratefully drove my vaccine partner home.

Stepping Out

JANE SPALDING

2021. As Joe and Kamala bring welcome change, as vaccines go into arms, and as soggy winter days slip into spring, the heavy blanket of 2020 grief begins to lift.

In March, my pandemic partner Nick and I move into a tiny rental house in Langley on Whidbey Island, my fourth move of the year. We begin to see his grandchildren more frequently. In April, my daughter Katie gets two shots, and we hug and cry. By May, mask mandates are in flux around the country. Schools and libraries open up. Restaurants offer indoor dining.

Is it safe to travel? I talk to my brother Joe in Santa Fe and we conjure up a visit. I want to explore parts of the Southwest and I'm thinking we have to drive. Joe says fly to Albuquerque, plan a slow drive to Salt Lake City and fly home. We decide to fly.

Anticipation is part of the fun of any trip. But this time planning is fraught with anxiety. Am I ready to crack open our safe pandemic cocoon to reenter the world? To be in three states, four national parks, and two airports? I plan anyway, and Nick says yes to every adventure I propose.

OK, we do it. Take the ferry to Seattle, leave the dog with friends, drive to SeaTac, fly to Albuquerque, rent a car, drive to Santa Fe. Seamless. No long lines anywhere. Everyone wears a mask. Is it my imagination or is the "general public" more kindhearted than in pre-pandemic times?

Now, back at home in Langley, we relive our adventure through Nick's 2,000 photographs, and the memories. Dining outdoors in Santa Fe's trademark restaurants. Cliff dwellings of the Ancestral Pueblo society with their architectural brilliance and focus on community. Days of deep blue sky with pasted on clouds. Miles and miles of rocks whose shapes and colors reflect eons of erosion into arches, canyons and otherworldly formations. So much magnificence. So different from Pacific Northwest splendor.

The highlight of the experience is people. My brother and his wife Mary show us their new home in the hills of Santa Fe. We visit my dear friend Louise who lost her husband John last year. And Posie, whose husband's health is declining, while she prepares to host a son's wedding at their home with a bride's family who refuses to be vaccinated. They remind me of the importance of showing up. And of hugs. No number of zoom experiences can substitute for hugs.

These are the people I know. Casual interactions with new people are richer after a shelter-in-place year. The woman taking a selfie in front of an arch of antlers at the entrance to Georgia O'Keefe's Ghost Ranch. Nick takes her photograph, and she exudes her love for the artist's work. Seven women have lunch at the Abiquiu Inn in New Mexico and plan a group painting exhibit. They remind me of the seven of us in my beloved writing group.

I remember a man doing a downward facing dog in the early morning on a rock in Arches National Park. The woman from Chicago who we encounter throughout our day at Canyonlands and her contagious joy at being there. The family from Michigan who share their picnic table with us as they explore Utah—with five children ages one to ten!

The climax is a young man who runs a thousand feet up to the top of a massive red boulder near the iconic Delicate Arch in Arches National Park. He waves his arms and yells to surprised onlookers below. We cheer in response—as if all gathered are celebrating—being healthy, being outside in a sacred space—because we can.

Brand New Year

TYSON GREER

On New Year's Day, I felt like the oxygen was flowing back into the room. The promise of leadership on the pandemic, social justice, and climate emergency felt like a new year.

On January 6th we were stunned—yes, insurrection *could* happen here in America.

Cable news benefited the most that day: 5,221,000 watched CNN; 4,006,000 stuck to MSNBC; 2,988,000 adhered to Fox News. We used to listen to the same news: Walter Cronkite, The Huntley-Brinkley Report, Dan Rather. Then in 1987, President Reagan's FCC abolished the Fairness Doctrine, and broadcast licensees were no longer required to devote airtime to honest, equitable, and balanced coverage of controversial issues. News then wasn't personalized or amplified by thrumming algorithms on social media. Nowadays, we each bear allegiance to our particular brand of news, not necessarily to the truth.

But the good times of 2021 had begun. Vaccines were available, but getting an appointment was hard; I finally got one for Jim, but not me. On a clear February night, a friend called at 10:07. "UW Medicine at Northgate has 300 doses and there's already 100 people in line—we'll pick you up." And we were off for a late-night vaccine party. After three hours stomping our feet in the cold, we were finally let inside, warm and humming strains from *Hamilton:* "We're gonna get our...shot." A nurse asked if anyone was willing to have their picture taken for the *Seattle Times*. No one raised a hand, so I did.

The next morning, my inbox brimmed with messages: "Hey Tyson, you and your arm made the cover of the *Seattle Times*!" I even heard from Beth in New Zealand and family in Canada. Media outlets around the world had picked up the "good news" story about how the medical community rallied after discovery of a broken freezer door and scrambled to bring back day-shift nurses and volunteers at three different facilities to put 1,650 vaccines in arms before the vaccines expired—not one shot was wasted!

In a Zoom interview with a local TV station, the reporter asked if I had gotten a polio shot (https://twitter.com/Q13FOXKiggins/status /1355303155307737089). Have you seen those 1950s photos of rows of kids in iron lungs? *Everybody* got a polio shot. In January 2019—a year before COVID-19—the World Health Organization identified the anti-vax movement as among the top ten global threats.

Spring of 2021, we entered the "post panic" pandemic period; we're living with it, not overwhelmed by it. In June, Jim and I could hug our fully vaccinated 14-year-old twin grandsons and their parents before they moved to North Carolina. There's other good news: The Keystone XL pipeline is officially dead, the Biden administration plans to restore protections of Alaska's Tongass National Forest, and we're no longer in the grip of hourly tweets.

However, one year after the murder of George Floyd there are more shootings and killings. Fourteen states have passed 22 restrictive voting laws—61 more such bills are advancing in 18 states—and the Supreme Court just backed Arizona's laws that discriminate against minority voters. The conspiracy theories continue to flourish. "The Big Lie" still has life. At the QAnon conference in Texas (The God & Country Patriot Roundup), a man in the audience asked Trump's former national security advisor Michael Flynn "why what happened in Myanmar [a coup] can't happen here?" The crowd roared approval when Flynn answered, "No reason, I mean, it should happen here."

I mourn the loss of civility and fear for the demise of our democracy. Beneath the happy hum of a new administration, the thrumming of discontent and disaffected people continues to rise.

We have work to do.

An 83-Year-Old Woman Who Lives Alone

MARY ANN GONZALES

Aftermath (noun): the Period Immediately Following an Unusually Ruinous Event

You wake up in the morning with a pain in the left side of your chest that carries down into your left arm. Now, everything you know about this symptom is that immediately you call 911. But, of course, that is not what you do. You get up, have breakfast and talk to yourself about what you should do. By afternoon when the symptoms have not diminished, you have decided that you really must do something, so you plan to go to the clinic. You gather up your keys, remind yourself that you have on clean underwear and go out to the car. At about that time you remember your daughter lives about 4 blocks away, so you call her, ask if she is busy. When you find she is cleaning out her car—you say, "This is about the most stupid thing I am ever going to say to you in your entire life, but I think I am having a heart attack, are you busy..." you have to stop talking because she is pulling up in front of your house. She tells you that the ER is faster than the clinic and so you go there.

Together you walk into the ER and find the lobby filled with people hunched in chairs looking miserable. When you quietly say "pain in my chest," the room becomes electric and people start coming out of nearby doors. You are whisked off while your daughter argues that she should stay with you, but they are adamant that she cannot. "COVID protocol," they say.

You are accompanied by three men, one says "My name is..., I will be your nurse. Will you please take off your clothes above the waist." You do as you are instructed and you are soon hooked to several machines, they look at monitors, go in and out of the room. Another man comes in tells you his name, sits down and says he will be your doctor. He asks a lot of questions and leaves.

During the lulls you begin a conversation with the male nurse. Chit-chat about working in this pandemic. Says he just moved here and bought a home nearby. Turns out, this man for whom you just removed your clothes, just bought a house around the corner from you. You decide to be an adult and not change the route of your daily walk.

For the next three hours you get massive attention: swallow nitroglycerin, have your blood taken, get your chest x-rayed while never leaving the bed, get wheeled upstirs for a CT-scan. The doctor comes back and says everything looks good you can go home. "Just take it easy" he cautions.

A woman from the front office comes in and says there will be a $50 co-pay do you want to put it on a card? On the way out your do just that. Your daughter is waiting, the car is in front and we leave.

You have just had thousands of dollars of medical attention and are reminded how enormously lucky you are to have insurance that much of the world does not have and so might not have gone to find medical help. And, you are not having a heart attack! But wonder how to "take it easy" when stress is the way of the world in the Time of COVID.

Out of the Woods

LAURA CELISE LIPPMAN

and after
life goes on with the usual diagnoses
low back pain, prostate,
streptococcus, childbirth,
hysterectomies, arthritis,
diabetes, dermatitis
HIV (the last great scourge)
and random viral ordinaries

no more stray Summer Tanagers
in backyard Seattle Christmas trees
mistaken for holiday ornaments
at this year's celebration.

back to the unremarkable
unexceptional, but
still somewhat memorable,
stifled by dailiness
with the unmitigated lurking fear
of one lethal variant or another.

So It Was Written

LAURA CELISE LIPPMAN

We believe the tides
   are inevitable
     and unchanging.

On the verge
   of losing
     our idealism

crafted long ago
   by a cabal of slave owners
     and romantics

whose avaricious compromise
   may now be
     our undoing

we mourn the loss
   of light and hope
     as legislators and electors

drone their way
   to the end
     of our sweet, shared dream.

The tides springs higher
   and ebb lower
     rivers of sea lettuce

flow to the sea
   as the earth turns
     and burns and burns.

Pause, Reset, Forward

SUZANNE TEDESKO

After a pandemic year of political mayhem and personal stasis, I couldn't wait to leave 2020 behind. Unfortunately, 2021 stormed in with the shocking January 6 assault on the Capitol meant to prevent President Biden from taking office. Like millions of Americans, I was shaken to the core by this blatant repudiation of the democratic process. Thankfully, Inauguration Day, set against the stirring backdrop of 200,000 flags along the Mall that stood in for citizens who in a normal year would attend, proceeded two weeks later without incident. The early days of the new administration signaled stability and a return to calm. It appeared that sanity would prevail.

I learned from my year on 'pause' how important having a sense of purpose is to my well-being. Given the rollout of two efficacious vaccines, I would be able to offer support to our overwhelmed daughter and her family and help care for our grandchildren. Although we lived only a short walk away, for nine months we'd seen them only outside, masked and social-distanced.

And so, come late February with my second vaccination, I could hug four-year-old Skyler again and hold baby Bodie, who at age one was on the move physically and verbally with language skills erupting like popcorn. Bodie's first words, "Cool," and "Wow," seemed particularly apt given the elation of being together at last.

But seeing other people? The introvert in me had gained ascendancy. *I'll have NOTHING to talk about. And what do I wear after a year of sweatpants, slouchy, bra-less tops and Crocs or old sneakers?* I opened the closet to assess my wardrobe trying to recall what blouses, pants, shoes and accessories went together. Eventually, after settling upon a few outfits, I tried on a favorite pair of jeans only to snag folds of flesh into the zipper. Apparently, under those baggy clothes, my body had changed: gravity had triumphed. So be it, I told myself. Get over it. The new me. 'Reset.'

Springtime brought a spate of glorious weather and whatever hint of social anxiety I'd felt earlier evaporated. Jubilant as sprites, my husband and I celebrated our first indoor dinner with vaxxed friends amidst candlelight and roses, hugs, laughter and champagne. Other pleasures would follow. Hiking in the rainforest. Slurping soft ice cream in a reopened mountain town. Kayaking down the Duwamish River. Soon we'll attend a twice-postponed destination wedding in the Methow Valley with the bride and groom, new parents of a three-month-old daughter.

We are now fully enmeshed with our daughter's family who moved in with us in April as they put their house on the market and prepared for an unexpected move to Arizona. Sadly, our multi-generational bubble of noisy, chaotic togetherness will soon end. In a matter of weeks my husband and I will caravan with them to their new home in Prescott and bid them *adios*...for now.

Moving from a full-bellied feast of family time to an empty nest will require major realignment. Time for me to direct my energy outward. Owing to trumped-up charges of election fraud in November, the rift in our country has deepened. Mass shootings and violence against minorities are on the rise and a rabid backlash has resulted in restrictive voting laws in a number of States. In Texas an obstructive abortion law flouts Roe v. Wade while a Florida law outlawing gatherings of three or more people without a specific permit challenges our Constitutional right of assembly. There is much to be done, but whatever personal path I take forward, one thing is clear: never again will I take for granted my freedom of movement, good health and ability to engage with the world.

All About Us

MARY ANN GONZALES

When my five children were teenagers, the City of Seattle launched the Forward Thrust program. Through this initiative, I along with several neighbors established the Ballard Community School. We polled the neighborhood for interests/wants and held night classes as a response to those requests. I was the director of this effort for five years until the Red Cross asked to add our classes to their roster.

At Antioch University, Seattle I helped establish a Community Development Program with the same intent but with a city-wide component. In this case we brought experts from around the world to lecture to students. At one of those events I met a man with AIDS.

Eventually I organized what was known as the first "public" AIDS informational event in Seattle.

The fledging Seattle AIDS Support Group accepted me as a support group leader and for 17 years I met once a week with Caregivers of People with AIDS. For a short time I had a private practice but found the group experience was more effective in managing these issues.

The American Red Cross was tasked with developing education programs to prepare and support organizations adapting to the facts of AIDS. I soon was lecturing at school and businesses. The Red Cross also supported the production of an AIDS film eventually shown on PBS and I was inordinately proud to see my name in the credits.

It became apparent to me that AIDS caregivers had no organization that spoke to their specific needs. I called together a group of experts and the AIDS Caregivers Support Network was born. We offered workshops and events that spoke to those individual needs. I was the director of this organization for the first few years.

Multiple Sclerosis Society hired me to manage and support their extensive support group program. This meant I traveled around Washington state to bring a personal presence and information to these sometimes far-flung groups that helped each other with the physical and emotional issues of MS.

I retired when my husband got cancer and I was able to use all that acquired caregiver knowledge to practical use.

Once I figured out I couldn't make daydreaming a profession, I shambled into the arts, broadly defined. But how did a nice gal from the city of Baltimore begin writing fiction set in the ranch lands of Idaho? It's all my friends' fault.

The summer we turned twelve, my best friend Betsey went out West with her parents for vacation. For a whole month. I fumed in Baltimore, which was then and still is hot and humid, unless you went to the ocean, which we sometimes did. I haunted the local library, lolled in the hammock reading countless books, rode horses (English style), wrote stories, went swimming, drew the cat, and pulled weeds. (The latter was not my idea.)

When Betsey returned, she told me about the horses and the cowboys, the big skies and the cowboys, the mountains and the cowboys... Then I grew up.

After hopscotching across the country, living in New Mexico, New York, Nevada—I was running out of states that started with "N"—and a year rambling around Europe on the back of a Triumph motorcycle with the kids (then five and eight) in a sidecar; Seattle seemed like a nice place to stay. Mountains, water, arts community (not a "scene")—not a lot of cowboys, but a good place to live and raise a family.

Just like living in different places, I've lived through different art forms: painting, sculpture, video, interactive media. Few things are as invigorating as change. Along the way, I created a checkerboard past that doesn't even remotely resemble a career. Except for a few short stints (e.g., museums and Microsoft), I earned a living by hiring myself.

"Tyson Greer....Writes" wrote and directed corporate television and documentaries, taught screenwriting, freelanced magazine articles, authored a nonfiction book for Microsoft (sold in eight languages) and ghosted or edited a couple others. And got to travel a lot. Then, cofounding a company to write learning technologies market analysis research reports with another Microsoft ex-pat, I got to travel to Asia and the Middle East.

It takes only a couple hours for my husband Jim and I to travel to our shanty-cabin perched on the North Fork of the Skykomish River—no running water, no electricity, but plenty of river. At home, although I still don't like weeding, I like growing things in the garden, harassing (encouraging) our little town to protect our enviable forest and dwindling salmon, plus dancing with Jim (my sweet Alberta man who wears cowboy boots). And traveling.

Travel. That's what took me to Idaho, my cowgirl friends the Lynn sisters, riding western, and a horse sale...

WANDA HERNDON

Oftentimes, a wide smile spreads across my face and I toss my head back while releasing a laugh that makes people look around to find the origin of the exuberant sound. I can find the humor in just about anything, except what's awful. Then I try to help. I am truly blessed, and I proudly give back to others who I am able to assist.

Though I fight the urge to fill every moment of each day with activities, I seem to be in perpetual motion. I have lost count of the number of times I have been complimented on my high energy, sense of humor and infectious laughter. That is just who I am, until I am not. Sometimes, situations require an extremely direct and honest response, so I deliver.

I run fast and hard so you might think I am running from something. I am actually running to something! And 99 percent of time I sprint forward; I am happy, a signature characteristic; I love to laugh; I love to create; I love to write. I discovered this when I was a little Black girl with big dreams, growing up in Flint, Michigan.

My foray into writing started in the 8th grade at Whittier Junior High School. When I was a 13, I wrote my first poem, *Discontent*, which I was asked to read on a children's radio program. After that initial success, I nurtured my love of the written word with bachelor's and master's degrees in journalism from Michigan State University. I was lucky enough to eventually be awarded an honorary doctor of humanities degree from my alma mater.

My obvious delight in being alive sometimes masks the more serious, brainy side of my personality, which can surprise those who underestimate me.

Along my journey, I figured out how to transition my writing skills into a corporate public relations career in Fortune 500 companies. Although I never fit the stereotype of a corporate executive, I ascended to executive positions at Dow Chemical, DuPont, and Starbucks. When Starbucks recruited me in 1995 for the top communications position, I didn't think that twenty-five years later I would still reside in Seattle, Washington, where I am actively engaged with the business and philanthropic communities while enjoying a wonderful life with great friends and opportunities.

"Stepping out on faith" when facing challenges is a constant battle cry in the African American community. It is the rule and not the exception for me. This explains how I became a producer of Tony Award-winning Broadway plays, *Memphis: The Musical* and *Come from Away*. These opportunities and others were unexpected and enriching! I am grateful.

Now, I have come full circle and remember my 13-year-old self, the girl with a zest for life who dared to dream. These days in retirement, I am writing my memoir, *Deadlocks in the Boardroom* and penning poetry that reflects my cultural observations, such as "I Cry," which was featured in the *Seattle Times*!

I am moving forward with hope and joy!

www.wcommgroup.com

LAURA CELISE LIPPMAN

Now, I call myself a poet. Honestly, all my physician father wanted for me, the oldest, was to become a doctor. So I succumbed. Yes, I loved reading, yes I loved being outside, but from early on there was one clear path...I had no interest in poetry as a girl, though my parents could recite many poems by heart. My rebellion against dad was to try to go into field biology, but when the acceptance to U. Cal Berkeley grad school in biology arrived with no stipend, and dad offered to fund a medical education, off to medical school I went. It helped that it was 1971, and the women's movement was blossoming. I had taken one of the first women's study courses at Bryn Mawr College taught by the famous Kate Millet (yes, if you remember, she debated Norman Mailer about Women's Lib on TV...), and it seemed almost *reactionary* not to devote one's life to women learning about their bodies and achieving equal recognition and treatment in the health care world.

I attended the Medical College of Pennsylvania. Formerly the Women's Medical College, it was forced to become coed to receive funds from the feds, because single sex med schools did not qualify for federal funding. Ah, one of life's many ironies.

I had come to the Pacific Northwest from the East Coast for my junior year, and I fell in love with the ocean, the mountains, the tide pools full of the most beautiful and interesting creatures. When I finally finished the torture that was medical school, I ended up in Seattle for a residency in family practice, then went into private practice in the North Seattle area for 35 years. I became interested in medical administration, in spite of myself. After practicing all that time, the insurance company grind finally did me in. I retired relatively early and moved on to my next life adventure. Along the way I was lucky enough to have a wonderful husband and two children. My physician spouse worked part time. My children have had their own children and chose to live near us.

With retirement, the fun started; I dabbled in so many areas I had not been able to experience; medical practice for low income folks, for the Navajo and Zuni tribes in Arizona, doctor for staff and students on the around the world voyage of the Semester at Sea, native plant steward certification, forest steward, citizen scientist studying fish eggs and seastar epidemics. Travel and writing classes were so rewarding. Somehow I found my way into two groups of stellar writers. I started writing poems. I could use my experiences in natural history, biology and ecology as well as life experiences to write, write, write and share my experiences, dividing my time between Seattle and Vashon Island.

How lucky am I.

My poems have appeared in Crosswinds, Pontoon Poetry, Mobius, *and* The Journal of Social Change *among other journals. I contributed a chapter to* On The Cable, *a 1972 report by the Sloan Foundation and various medical publications.*
https://www.laura-celise-lippman-poetry.com

JANE SPALDING

I grew up in Kentucky and slowly worked my way to the Pacific Northwest corner of our country.

I've become one of those people who can't live without water nearby.

I grew up in the days when I could aspire to be a teacher, a mother, a nurse, or a nun. I choose teacher, after earning a master's degree in a federally funded program called the Teacher Corps. After seven years of teaching I discovered non-profit organizations, a world I didn't know existed, again through a federally funded program.

The Evansville Arts and Education Council hired me, who knew nothing about how to do the job, to be executive director. That led to twenty incredibly rewarding years raising money for hospitals. The most exciting of all was as Harborview Medical Center's director of development. In 2015, I retired from Seattle University, where for ten years I had the privilege of serving as director of corporate and foundation relations.

Travel has been an underlying urge throughout my life. The desire to see the world led me to find a teaching job in Milan, Italy, when I was 23, to see much of the United States, to take a trip to Japan, and to spend time in Mexico and Zimbabwe.

My most significant trip was in 1995 when I went to China and came home with a baby girl. Katherine Mei Xia Spalding became my spirit guide. In fact, it was wanting to write the story of my trip to China that inspired me to seek out a writing group. And what a wonderful group I found!

Since I retired, I've enjoyed doing volunteer consulting work for small non-profit organizations. For now, I'm content to share life between Seattle and Whidbey Island with my "shelter in place" companion Nick.

SUZANNE TEDESKO

I was raised in a New York suburb and graduated from a women's college in Massachusetts. The summer after college, as I sat on the lip of a Kentucky strip mine wondering what to do with a philosophy degree, I had an epiphany: education was the answer and film, the medium. I spent the next five years in New York City as a documentary film researcher and associate producer on subjects that included the Puerto Rican community, a history of the Jews, and refugees from Eastern Europe.

When Smithsonian Institution offered me a job as program director of a six-month long Folklife Festival for Expo '74, I was intrigued. My research skills would transfer easily to programming 26 ethnic mini-festivals on the three-acre site. The catch: the job required a temporary move to Spokane, Washington. Ready for an adventure, I found my way to the Pacific Northwest and decided to stay. After Expo, I moved to Seattle and returned to film and video work at KCTS/9, producing two documentaries that aired nationally over PBS stations.

Perhaps having an Austrian father seeded my abiding interest in other cultures. While the venues for my work over the years have ranged from documentary film, video and radio production to ethnographic research and writing, refugee work and citizen diplomacy, the theme of cultural identity has suffused much of it. In 2006 I completed a post-graduate degree in cross-cultural communication from the Center for World Indigenous Studies in Olympia, Washington. I've travelled extensively, circumnavigating the globe twice on

"Semester at Sea"; our family also lived in New Zealand, Fiji and Barbuda during my husband's sabbaticals.

In recent years I've turned my attention to writing, with three editions of a Seattle guidebook for Fodors and a screenplay, "Swimming Upstream." I'm currently completing a first novel. My two grown children, their partners and our four adorable grandchildren are my pride and joy.

BETH WEIR

I am New Zealander by birth or as we are known colloquially, a Kiwi. My husband and I moved to the United States in 1976 with two babies in tow, expecting to stay five years. Those initial years have grown into almost five decades.

The first thirty years we spent in Raleigh, North Carolina, exploring the riches, humor, warts, and eccentricities of the South; an education all by itself. For some of that time I worked at a sturdy little institution called Meredith College that has served women for over one hundred years. My role as a professor of education, and the chance it provided to explore an interest in literacy acquisition, gave me immense pleasure.

My unexpected retirement came in 2005 when my husband was offered a job in Seattle. We drove across country in a five-day snowstorm and crossed the I-90 Bridge at 3:30 p.m.in the rapidly darkening, rainy, December afternoon. Such was my welcome to the Pacific Northwest. Despite the inauspicious start, the region has proved itself most hospitable. The fact I now live as I did growing up in New Zealand, in close proximity to water and mountains, helps.

It turned out my working life wasn't finished as I served, unexpectedly and happily for five years, as the executive director of the Dunn Gardens in the north of Seattle. For an enthusiastic gardener such as myself, going to work was like going to Eden.

I am writing in my retirement. I cannot claim it is always fun but the enterprise has robust benefits. One of them is having good writing friends. It turns out they are good friends too.

We are always awake to mindful sayings about writing. This is my favorite for the year of 2020.

"Write what should not be forgotten." —Isabel Allende

As a group we are trying to do that.

Final Note

BETH WEIR

It has been my pleasure to compile this book about the experience of living through COVID-19.

What started as individual expression—writing of the challenges we each navigated—brought us together while we have been apart. My thanks to the members of my writing sisterhood for making this project easy:

Mary Ann Gonzales is our oldest member who is good-quirky and a role model for us all about aging well. (Basically, this means, not appearing to do so at all.) Besides working on this project, Mary Ann has an epistolary book on the boil about the Japanese Internment Camps during WWII through the experiences of both the interned and those who managed their stay.

Wanda Herndon is our wonderfully cheerful, energizer bunny who has inspired us all by her life and zest for new experiences. Wanda has had an exceptional career and is in the *n*th iteration of inventing herself after her corporate life. While she is a particular role model for Black women she serves as one for everyone else as well. She has almost finished her memoir, *Dreadlocks in the Boardroom*.

Tyson Greer lives life joyously and right to the edges, besides managing all things technical. She generously helps us all with our glitches and anything else she can. In my case that meant helping me understand sourdough starter. Tyson will soon send her second novel set in Idaho off to her agent. It will make a cowgirl out of the slickest of city slickers.

Laura Celise Lippman is our primary poet. No one knew a published poet before we knew Laura, so she is regarded with awe. As we critique her work, she teaches us about the art form and to appreciate its nuances. She is also a retired physician and is more than generous with her time when we bring her our woes around aging. Laura is currently compiling a collection of her superb poems.

Jane Spalding is relatively new to the group and doubts her writing abilities; an emotion not justified as you will see by her entries. Jane has this ability to take the messes of life along with their simple joys and make them interesting and universal. She is finding her way as a writer and we look forward to what is next.

Suzanne Tedesko is our compassionate cheerleader and grammarian. Those of us who find commas superfluous are grateful for her steady eye. She is a meticulous researcher and the novel she is about to finish reflects that. As we are all of a certain age, we remember the experiences that Suzie describes and cringe at the description of it as being a period piece. Are we really that old?

Beth Weir: I recently completed a novel centered around a woman who has recently retired, and it is now with an enthusiastic agent. Writing it kept me from fretting too much about COVID-19. It is my hope a reader will enjoy the story in a world that is no longer menaced by the virus.

Living through COVID-19 has changed and chastened us. We are grateful that none of the group lost a family member or a friend to the disease and are mindful that was a privilege not afforded all.

We hope you enjoyed our considerations of 2020 and beyond.

Index